'Alternative' Cultures and Leisure

Contemporary discourse on sustainability points to the need for substantial, if not radical, shifts in relations between productivity, environment, consumption and identities, in ways which bring or restore balance to the intersecting domains. The catchphrase of 'sustainability' has made its way into mainstream discourse on the heels of the ongoing global financial crisis and in response to global warming. The literature of leisure, sport and particularly tourism are replete with fine examples of 'sustainability', contributing to full ecology planning approaches.

This book aims to stimulate debate and discussion within the leisure studies community about the roles of 'alternative cultures' in producing viable models of sustainable relations between work, leisure and environment. Key elements of these discussions, such as participatory democracy and deep ecology, have long been characteristic of cultural configurations loosely called 'counter' or 'alternative' to a voracious, hierarchical and unconscious modernity. However, the leisure studies community has largely neglected their significance up until now. How are leisure, sustainable livelihoods and 'alternative' cultures connected, and what influence do they have?

This book was originally published as a special issue of *Annals of Leisure Research*.

Alan Law is an Associate Professor of Sociology at Trent University, Peterborough, Ontario, Canada. His research agendas range across a number of sociological sub-disciplines and methodologies. His interests in the sport and leisure field currently focus on the impact of tourist resorts on local communities.

Stephen L. Wearing is an Associate Professor in the UTS Business School at the University of Technology, Sydney, Australia. He has conducted numerous projects and lectures worldwide, and is the author of 13 books and over 100 articles dealing with issues surrounding leisure and sustainable tourism.

'Alternative' Cultures and Leisure

Creating pathways for sustainable livelihoods

Edited by
Alan Law and Stephen L. Wearing

Routledge
Taylor & Francis Group

LONDON AND NEW YORK

First published 2015 by Routledge

2 Park Square, Milton Park, Abingdon, Oxon OX14 4RN
711 Third Avenue, New York, NY 10017, USA

Routledge is an imprint of the Taylor & Francis Group, an informa business

First issued in paperback 2017

British Library Cataloguing in Publication Data
A catalogue record for this book is available from the British Library

ISBN 13: 978-1-138-91358-5 (hbk)
ISBN 13: 978-1-138-08282-3 (pbk)

Typeset in Times New Roman
by diacriTech, Chennai

Publisher's Note
The publisher accepts responsibility for any inconsistencies that may have arisen during the conversion of this book from journal articles to book chapters, namely the possible inclusion of journal terminology.

Disclaimer
Every effort has been made to contact copyright holders for their permission to reprint material in this book. The publishers would be grateful to hear from any copyright holder who is not here acknowledged and will undertake to rectify any errors or omissions in future editions of this book.

Contents

Citation Information

The chapters in this book were originally published in the *Annals of Leisure Research*, volume 17, issue 3 (October 2014). When citing this material, please use the original page numbering for each article, as follows:

Please direct any queries you may have about the citations to
clsuk.permissions@cengage.com

Notes on Contributors

Cris Calley Jones is a Clinical Social Worker in private practice. No longer conducting academic research, her professional interests include working with families in conflict, mediation and psychotherapy. She continues to engage social change through leisure interests.

Stuart Gifford is a co-founder and co-owner of Sarah's Sister's Sustainable Café, Semaphore, Australia, and is an urban activist.

Freya Higgins-Desbiolles is a Senior Lecturer in Tourism with the School of Management of the University of South Australia, Adelaide, Australia. She is a critical tourism scholar, and is dedicated to a research agenda focusing on sustainability, human rights and social justice.

Jonathan Joseph is a University Medalist and Honours Graduate from the University of Technology, Sydney, Australia. He has a keen interest in various research areas, such as sustainable tourism, event and leisure management and popular culture.

Bernadett Kis is a psychologist working as an Assistant Professor at the Institute of Applied Health Sciences and Health Promotion at the University of Szeged, Hungary. She has been a member of a CSA initiative for two years.

Alan Law is an Associate Professor of Sociology at Trent University, Peterborough, Ontario, Canada. His research agendas range across a number of sociological sub-disciplines and methodologies. His interests in the sport and leisure field currently focus on the impact of tourist resorts on local communities.

Heather Mair is an Associate Professor at the University of Waterloo, Canada. Her research interests include investigations of food-related social movements, the politics of tourism, leisure and sport development in communities as well as critical approaches to social research.

Emily Moskwa is a researcher with the Centre for Regional Engagement of the University of South Australia, Adelaide, Australia.

Karl Spracklen is a Professor of Leisure Studies at Leeds Metropolitan University, UK. His latest book is *Leisure, Sport and Society*. He is the Principal Editor of the journal *Metal Music Studies*.

Stephen L. Wearing is an Associate Professor in the UTS Business School at the University of Technology, Sydney, Australia. He has conducted numerous projects and lectures worldwide, and is the author of 13 books and over 100 articles dealing with issues surrounding leisure and sustainable tourism.

INTRODUCTION

'Alternative' cultures and leisure: creating pathways for sustainable livelihoods

Alan Law[a] and Stephen L. Wearing[b]

[a]Sociology, Trent Applied Social Research Lab, Trent University, Peterborough, ON, Canada; [b]Management Discipline Group, UTS Business School, University of Technology, Sydney, Ultimo, Australia

This issue aims to stimulate debate and discussion within the leisure studies community about the roles of 'alternative cultures' in producing viable models of sustainable relations between work, leisure, and environment. Contemporary discourse on sustainability points to the need for substantial if not 'radical' shifts in relations between productivity, environment, consumption, and identities in ways that bring or restore its balance to intersecting domains. The catchphrase of 'sustainability' has arguably made its way into mainstream discourse on the heels of the recent recession and response to global warming. The leisure, sport, and particularly tourism literatures are replete with fine examples contributing to full ecology planning approaches. Key elements of these discussions such as participatory democracy and deep ecology have long been characteristic of cultural configurations loosely called 'counter' or 'alternative' to a voracious, hierarchical, and unconscious modernity; however, the leisure studies community has largely neglected their significance. How are leisure, sustainable livelihoods and alternative cultures connected and what influence do they have?

Social scientific scholarship on 'counter' and 'alternative' cultures has primarily centred on the 'hippie' social movements of the late 1960s, rural and urban communes and 'deviant' subcultures coalescing around music, street life, and ecological commitment. Contemporary rural and urban 'communes' and back to the land movements are prominent in many areas today attracting a younger generation to resist materialist hegemonies. There are many different ways that people today, through their leisure, travel, and sport, seek to acquire and even emulate 'alternative lifestyles.'

Theoretical traditions intersecting with these empirical domains have been diverse and include the work of the Frankfurt School, British style cultural studies, post-structuralist identity regulation, anthropological style ethnography, and more. The present papers make empirical, theoretical, or methodological contributions to ways in which 'alternative' cultural practices navigate and negotiate novel configurations of production/consumption relations. This is manifestly aimed at skirting key problems of modernity by reorganizing the temporality and spatiality of work/leisure binaries, reorganizing the priority of work and leisure as biographical guides, reorganizing ideas of social and distributive justice, and reorganizing relations between identity, consumption, and environment. Leisure is a central feature of the future of sustainability and also society, and an understanding of this is an essential ingredient for all policy-makers, academics, and service providers. Alternative cultures may be more than just odd aberrations. What kinds of keys might they hold to a better life?

Much of our inquiry into the alternative seeks critiques of mainstream consumer culture; as such we seek to move from the view of leisure providing a critique of work as in the past to drawing on insights from a more 'critical' perspective which is provided in the alternative voices in this edition. We suggest that by analysing the particular conditions that characterize 'late', 'multinational', or 'consumer' capitalism (Jameson 1991), where there has been a loss of an overarching moral authority which people can gravitate towards, and a foundation from which to anchor self-identity. There is room for the alternative as these circumstances have led to more fluid social groupings. So although consumer discourses have come to replace traditional institutions in Western society, providing a wider set of authorities to gravitate towards, we find in this challenge to the traditional notions of self-identity space for the alternative.

In this special issue, Karl Spracklen provides us with insights into the alternative music scene(s) since the 1980 with the idea of 'heat death' which refers to the loss of radical, alternative ideologies in leisure spaces and the simultaneous transformation of these spaces into individualized, commodified ones. We see the alternate becoming mainstream this follows the trends in many of our alternative spaces in a society that is dominated by consumer culture(s). He concludes that in its emerging role as one choice of individual identity inside the neoliberal machine, alternativeness becomes a matter of clothes, bands and choices, but loses its struggle to fight the system. The spaces left for real alternative leisure and culture in popular music are, as a consequence, very small.

Freya Higgins-Desbiolles, Emily Moskwa, and Stuart Gifford bring to the discussion the sustainability pedagogue around food in a space that appears to have been taken over by the TV food shows; we get some insights into how it can be different. The fights in one of the editors households alone emphasis this debate, our children are not allowed to watch the competitive cooking shows – I want the kitchen to be a place and space of peace and family not competition and the spectacular. Stuart Gifford, currently a co-owner of Sarah's Sister's Sustainable Café brings to life the counter-culture to the trends in popular food culture to gastronomic emptiness. The paper shows where the alternative paths may lie and why food is 'a sustainability issue' aligned to the Slow Food movement and the participants can be in a cooperative rather than solely consumer relationship.

This leads us to Bernadett Kis' paper on community-supported agriculture (CSA). With the growth in this area and related areas such as WWOOFing (Willing Works on Organic Farms), we are seeing the reestablishment of people, families, and leisure and tourism back into our food production. Bernadett suggests that CSA is a particular approach to the production and distribution of local food. It is based on the direct connection between a nearby farmer and people who eat what the farmer has produced. A link in a consumer world that has separated us from the production of food and has allowed Woolworths to become the biggest promoter of its fresh food – 'Woolworths Australia's Fresh Food People' ad campaign (see http://www.woolworths.com.au/wps/wcm/connect/webSite/Woolworths/) in a consumer culture the warnngs signs are automatic why do they need an ad campaign to promote fresh food, have you ever brought fruit, vegetables or meat and seafood at Woolworths – if you have you would know why they need such an extensive and expensive ad campagin. 'The carrots are crisp, tasty and sometimes crooked. You wouldn't find them on the shelves at Woolworths; and that's the point' (Milla and Fyfe 2012, 1). And here lies the crux of the current selling in consumer culture – advertsing does not have to represent the truth only a market strategy, it has fundamental flaws focused on the selling of the brand. In Kis' paper, we have an alternative to the leisure of the mass detached consumption of the shopping mall, a way to make connections and genuinely establish a relationship to our food production and producers, a farmer who is accountable to a customer and this we are told is largely responsible for the emergence of other local agricultural forms like farmers' markets and community gardens.

Chris Calley Jones and Heather Mair bring the magical back to activism and what better way than through the idea of witch camps. They bring us a 'notion of magical activism (*which*) captures both the experience of the participants and the connection between personal and social transformation.' Not since the days of Edward Abby's 'The Monkey Wrench Gang' and Peter Singer 'Animal Liberations' have we seen new ways of exploring how we can be an activist in a consumer dominated society. This paper steps away from the technical in alternative culture and brings back the spirituality of Gaia, but in a robust research framework. It suggests that leisure can evolve a new activism through the creation of safe and sacred spaces, the witch camp and these participants may obtain raised consciousness, personal transformation, while also enhancing their political and social justice efficacy.

Finally, we arrive at the ultimate venture for Western consumer culture and its subsequent lifestyle, tourism. Jonathan Joseph and Stephen Wearing bring popular culture and TV together to examine how the popular culture celebrities can be linked to alternative tourism. This paper examines the influence that popular culture and travel engagements have on Generation Y. These two areas of leisure activity shape social and cultural norms and influence the construction of self-identity amongst this group. The paper highlights some areas where popular culture and alternative tourism can be valued as constructive factors influencing Generation Y. The focus of the research is on popular culture celebrity 'Bear' Grylls and his TV show 'Man vs. Wild' and the effect it had on the alternative tourism engagements of Generation Y 'gappers.'

References

Jameson, F. 1991. *Postmodernism, or, the Cultural Logic of Late Capitalism*. Durham, NC: Duke University Press.

Milla, R., and M. Fyfe. 2012. *Food from Somewhere, Foodwise: Your Site for Sustainable Food*. Accessed July 31 2014. http://www.foodwise.com.au/food-from-somewhere/.

There is (almost) no alternative: the slow 'heat death' of music subcultures and the instrumentalization of contemporary leisure

Karl Spracklen

Carnegie Faculty, Leeds Metropolitan University, Leeds, UK

In this paper, the metaphor of the 'heat death' is used in understanding the transformation of the alternative music scene(s) since the 1980s. Popular music is a key leisure space of modernity, and has been used as a space for negotiations of identity, conformity and transgression. Since the 1960s, alternative popular music has shaped the evolution of an authentic, communicative counter-cultural leisure space. The paper uses new research on online fan communities of black metal and extreme metal, and goth and post-punk, to demonstrate that the ideal of the alternative music scene as a communicative leisure space is not matched by the reality of the instrumentalization of contemporary leisure. Rather, there has been a slow metaphorically entropic shift in alternative music, from a shared subcultural and counter-cultural leisure space into one part of a globalized entertainment industry that has colonized the Habermasian lifeworld of leisure.

Introduction

When nineteenth-century scientists formulated the Laws of Thermodynamics, the second law showed that entropy would increase and lead to the slow 'heat death' of everything in the universe. Smith and Wise have shown that the concepts of thermodynamics discovered by James Maxwell (later Lord Kelvin) were shaped in part by 'conceptual and material resources available in his industrial culture, and with motivations shaped by that culture' (Smith and Wise 1989, xx). The idea of the 'heat death' of the universe became a popular subject of newspapers, magazines and books in the late nineteenth century, as people inside and outside the community of natural science discussed the implications of the universe running out of steam (Whitworth 1998). The idea quickly became a metaphor for the decline of civilizations and empires (MacDuffie 2011; Smith and Wise 1989; Whitworth 1998). In this paper, the metaphor of the 'heat death' is used in understanding the transformation of the alternative music scene(s) since the 1980s – specifically, heat death refers to the loss of radical, alternative ideologies in leisure spaces and the simultaneous transformation of these spaces into individualized, commodified ones.

Popular music is a key leisure space of modernity, and has been used as a space for negotiations of identity, conformity and transgression (Bennett 2000, 2006; Brill 2008; Hebdige 1979; Hodkinson 2002; Kahn-Harris 2007). From its origins, popular music has been a leisure industry, controlled by the instrumental logic of capitalism, and part of the wider entertainment industry (Lashua, Spracklen, and Wagg 2014; Spracklen 2013).

But popular music is shaped by the agency of fans, journalists and musicians. Popular music is talked about, listened to and consumed by fans – people who identify with the genres they listen to, or the artists themselves (Bennett 2000; Hodkinson 2002). Popular music is written about by journalists and by fans in their leisure time. At the same time, others construct popular music as part of their own leisure lives as amateur, semi-professional musicians and producers (Hesmondhalgh 2006). Popular music spaces are sites of leisure: leisure forms, practices, identities and behaviours. As such, they could be argued to be spaces for agency, resistance and what Spracklen (2009, 2011, 2013), following Habermas (1984, 1987), calls communicative leisure. Since the 1960s, alternative popular music has shaped the birth and evolution of an authentic, communicative counter-cultural leisure space (Bennett 2000). In the 1970s, Hebdige (1979) showed how a number of British youth subcultures constructed around style and popular music (such as mods and punks) were sites of counter-hegemonic resistance for marginalized (working-class) groups. But he also suggested, following the work of Gramsci (1971), that these subcultures were inevitably co-opted and drained of their transformative potential by hegemonic, mainstream culture.

The paper will draw on existing research by the author on goths and black/extreme metal (Lucas, Deeks, and Spracklen 2011; Spracklen 2006, 2012, 2013; Spracklen, Lucas, and Deeks 2014; Spracklen and Spracklen 2012, 2014), as well as new research undertaken by the author on the histories of the scenes and the scenes today online (fan communities and presence of black metal and extreme metal, and goth and post-punk), to demonstrate that the ideal of the alternative music scene as a communicative leisure space is not matched by the reality of the instrumentalization of contemporary leisure (Spracklen 2009, 2011). Rather, there has been a slow metaphorically entropic shift in alternative music, from a shared subcultural and counter-cultural leisure space – a space of direct political activism where potentiality and autonomy were possible – into one part of a globalized entertainment industry that has colonized the Habermasian lifeworld of leisure (Habermas 1984, 1987; Spracklen 2009, 2011). The paper will conclude by suggesting there are some small spaces within alternative music where communicative resistance may be possible, but there is little space for sustained political action. Before I discuss the two popular music scenes that are the focus of this research, I will briefly review the relevant literature and describe the methods I have used to understand and analyse those scenes.

Alternative leisure, alternative culture and oppositionality

Alternative leisure has been the subject of much research in leisure studies and the wider subject fields of sociology and cultural studies (Bennett 2006; Dilley and Scraton 2010; Fendt and Wilson 2012; Griggs 2012; Pavlidis 2012; Stebbins 2011). For some researchers, alternative leisure is about lifestyle and the neo-tribe, picking and choosing identities in the face of liquidity, postmodernity or globalization (Griggs 2012; Pavlidis 2012). In these analyses, alternative leisure becomes just another piece of positionality and performativity, much like dark leisure or deviant leisure (Rojek 2000). Clearly, the notion of alternative as neo-tribe is part of the neo-liberal individualism of contemporary leisure (Bennett 2000; Blackshaw 2010; Maffesoli 1996; Rojek 1995, 2000, 2010). But another way of thinking about alternative leisure is to understand the political underpinnings of alternativism, the oppositionality that was and is associated with alternative culture. This way, alternative leisure becomes a radical politics of young people, the working classes and others bereft of power, jobs and status, who find in the collective resistance of alternative leisure solace and communicative satisfaction (Debord 1995; Lefebvre 1991).

The idea of alternative culture demands an understanding of the hegemony of the mainstream. Gramsci (1971) and Adorno and Horkheimer (1992) demonstrate how popular culture or mainstream culture is constructed to keep the working classes and other marginalized groups in a state of perpetual disempowerment. Williams (1977, 1981) expands the concepts of hegemony and culture in great detail. In *Marxism and Literature* (Williams 1977) he develops a trifold relationship of culture. By culture it is taken to mean the cultural and ideological practices that pertain to a particular social group. At any one time hegemony produces a dominant culture, the culture which in contemporary society is taken as the template for good modes of behaviour and ideas. This is the 'culture' to which sections named so in newspapers refer to, things that are seen to have good aesthetic, intellectual and social power, such as classical music, literature, theatre and so on (Williams 1981). However, the hegemonic relationship means that this culture is dominant throughout all levels of society. Williams (1977) responds to this challenge by stating that – in opposition to the dominant – there will be cultural forms that are residual forms from the past, or emergent forms that may eventually challenge the hegemony. Hence, there are three power relationships, and culture can be represented as a contested dynamic. As we have seen, for Hebdige (1979), this Williamsian account of culture and hegemony describes the rise and fall of popular music and youth subcultures. This can also be understood in Habermasian terms. Subcultures begin as emergent forms of communicative resistance to the mainstream, but become accommodated and co-opted into the mainstream through a process of instrumental commodification.

Alternative culture is (or was) an emergent subculture associated with oppositionality (Lefebvre 1991; Martin 2004). Some theorists have identified alternativeness with the New Age movement (Wallis 2013). While the New Age movement might be seen as a part of a wider oppositional, counter-cultural turn, this is not how I intend to use the idea of alternativism. In this paper, I see alternativism as a political project of resistance to capitalism, with communicative oppositionality as its defining feature. In this, I follow the work of Spracklen, Richter, and Spracklen (2013, 168), who argue:

> Oppositionality is the way in which individuals, subcultures, counter-cultures and other counter-hegemonic movements reject the restrictions of instrumentality and express their refusal to conform as passive consumers … While it is clear that some people, pace Bourdieu, have the right cultural, social and economic capital to be successful opposition-alists (cf. Rojek 2010), the liberty to be able to act and to oppose is constrained by the enormous cultural, political and social powers of the instrumental structures ranged against freedom of expression and movement.

Methodology

This research paper follows on from previously published research by research colleagues and myself on the black metal and goth scenes as leisure spaces (Lucas, Deeks, and Spracklen 2011; Spracklen 2006, 2012, 2013; Spracklen, Lucas, and Deeks 2014; Spracklen and Spracklen 2012, 2014). Like these earlier research projects, this research is based on qualitative participant-observation within these scenes over many years, combined with formal virtual ethnography of six websites between 2009 and 2014. While virtual ethnography does limit me to English sources and those that are online, it does allow me to capture a sense of what people think about their scenes. My own insider reflections help me to situate the research and the history of the subcultures. I have used

Wikipedia and other public-generated online spaces as they reflect a certain level of general knowledge about the scenes – what people think these scenes are – even though sites such as Wikipedia are problematic as sources of 'truth'. The virtual ethnography and ethnographic reflections are combined with my knowledge of the scenes' histories to allow me to undertake the 'messy' analytical device of discourse tracing (LeGreco and Tracy 2009). I am a critical insider in both of these scenes and have been able to provide ethnographic reflections on both for the published research, and for this new research. The notion of the critical insider has been attacked by some methodologists and social theorists, who make the point that identity is always fluid, and boundaries between insiders and outsiders are always negotiated and spaces where power is at work (see especially Bennett 2002). Hodkinson (2005, 134) defends the concept of the 'insider' as researcher from those who attack it in the following way:

> Like most social science terminology, the notion of 'insider research' reduces complexities to generalities; but, through doing so, it establishes that researchers may sometimes find themselves positioned especially close to those they study and enables the tentative development of valuable common lessons about the probable implications of researching from such a position.

I am fortunate to have been a goth growing up in the 1980s in Leeds, the (supposedly) goth capital of England in the formative years of the goth scene, home of the key band The Sisters of Mercy, when post-punk was transforming into the goth music and subculture. I have maintained an interest in and connection to the goth scene both locally in the north of England and globally. I was also a metaller at the same time, crossing both scenes as many others did, finding a shared 'alternative' identity. I still remain a fan of heavy metal, especially the extreme metal sub-genres of black metal, pagan metal and doom, and like the goth scene, I have a connection to the extreme metal scene both locally and globally. So, *pace* Hodkinson, I feel myself positioned very favourably to the subjects of my research, and that close positionality enables me to write something *meaningful, yet, be critically evaluative* about these scenes and genres and their relationship to alternative leisure and cultures.

Histories of alternative cultures, ethnographies of commodified leisure

Goths in the 1980s and 1990s

The emergence of goth music and the associated scene was an accident of human agency and sub-cultural evolution and innovation. Punks growing bored with the rigid rules of the punk scene at the end of the 1970s started to experiment with new fashions in clothing and make-up, producing what became identified as a 'post-punk' look (Brill 2008; Hodkinson 2002; Martin 2004). Post-punk fashions continued into the early 1980s, and nightclubs held nights where people could explore post-punk styles. At the same time, a number of bands started to identify their sound as belonging to a post-punk genre, identifying with the ideology of punk, but experimenting with different sonic templates (Martin 2004). In the nightclubs, bands such as Bauhaus, the Banshees, the Southern Death Cult and Alien Sex Gang built up fan bases for their dark and exciting sounds. These bands in turn reached the pages of music magazines, where the post-punk term was coined (Hodkinson 2002; Martin 2004). In the UK, post-punk along with 'new wave' bands were touted as the next big thing by taste-setting music magazines such as *Sounds* and *New Musical Express*.

Some of the post-punk bands and fashions were labelled as gothic, a word borrowed from wider popular culture, because the sounds and lyrics channelled disillusionment among teenagers with the neo-liberalism of Margaret Thatcher and the lack of faith in the future. Gothic fashions were 'do-it-yourself' (DIY) post-punk fashions mixing and matching colours and cast-offs, not the all-black uniform of goth fashions in later years (Brill 2008; Hodkinson 2002). Goth music was part of the underground punk and rock subcultures, and goth bands played events alongside indie-pop bands. In Leeds, the Sisters of Mercy were formed by Andrew Eldritch among the indie-pop, student-pop spaces of the Headingley (Leeds 6) university district. The band soon developed a reputation for its dark, dance-friendly pop, with the use of drum machines, jangly guitars, synthesizers and groovy bass-lines. The band was at the vanguard of the popularization of goth, and established the goth template of black clothing, leather, bleakness, snakebite and dry ice that a thousand other bands (and fans) copied. But Eldritch used the band's fame to espouse left-wing politics, and true to the ideology of punk the band ran its own affairs and its own label. In its early days, then, the goth scene and genre served to describe and delineate a communicative and alternative leisure space, just like punk in the 1970s. Goth had, then, a radical ideology of alternativism.

As the 1980s progressed, goth bands, goth fans, goth pubs and goth nightclubs were part of a wider alternative music scene, with goths mixing with punks and metallers. Alternative scenes in the UK and Europe embraced a plurality of musical styles, connected only by the thread of a radical ideology inherited from punk of anti-consumerism and anti-mainstream (Spracklen and Spracklen 2012, 2014). Even as bands signed to major labels and bands appeared that had changed their fashions and music to sound more gothic, the communicative nature of the alternative scene remained strong. People identified with alternativism and equated gothness with a commitment to alternative politics and positions, an identity that came to shape the 'dark' scene in mainland Europe into this century (Hodkinson 2002; Spracklen and Spracklen 2014). Into the 1990s, this alternative identity was fractured in the UK, as goth music's key taste-makers grew old, changed their identities or were sacked from music magazines (Hodkinson 2002). The goth scene continued to exist but on a much smaller scale, taking strong influences from the dance music scene. At this time in the USA, the goth subculture started to be identified with fans of bands, such as Marilyn Manson, and erroneous conflations were made between goths and metallers (Spracklen and Spracklen 2012, 2014). Goths came to be identified in American popular culture (in movies and television programmes such as *South Park*) as suicidal outcasts in black clothes, dangerous to themselves but mostly harmless (unless there was a moral panic about murderers; see Griffiths 2010).

Goths in the 2000s and 2010s

In this century, goth has become an accepted form of subculture, both for young people choosing an 'alternative' identity and for older people continuing to express a feeling of subcultural identity through declaring themselves (still) to be goths (Hodkinson 2011, 2013; Spracklen and Spracklen 2012, 2014). In the mainstream of popular culture, goths are mixed up with emos and metallers (see the discussion about abuse against these in Garland 2010). Online information about goths is found on thousands of websites. Searching for 'goth' on Google brings up the information provided by Wikipedia and other popular sites. Wikipedia suggests that 'the Goth subculture has survived much longer than others of the same era, and has continued to diversify. Its imagery and cultural proclivities indicate influences from the nineteenth-century Gothic literature along with horror films' (http://en.wikipedia.org/wiki/Goth_subculture). The survival and diversification of goth is obviously true. More debatable is the confusion between the goth music scene and Gothic literature and Gothic horror (see the critique in Spracklen and Spracklen 2014). They are influences now because people have confused goth with Gothic, but in its original post-punk communicative leisure state, such connections were never explicitly intended. On fashion, Wikipedia provides a separate page with pictures of modern goths dressing up (http://en.wikipedia.org/wiki/Gothic_fashion, accessed 4 February 2014):

> Gothic fashion is a clothing style marked by conspicuously dark, mysterious, exotic, and complex features. It is worn by members of the goth subculture. A dark, sometimes morbid fashion and style of dress, typical gothic fashion includes a pale complexion with colored black hair, black lips and black clothes. Both male and female goths wear dark eyeliner and dark fingernail polish. Styles are often borrowed from the punks, Victorians and Elizabethans. Goth fashion is sometimes confused with heavy metal fashion and emo fashion.

For Wikipedia, goth fashion is carefully delineated and defined, and one can simply follow the instructions and the pictures to dress like a goth. That is, goth has become simply one other part of commodified popular culture. Goths are not Satanists, or anarchists, or squatters, or radicals; they are reduced to a set of instructions about what to wear, a vague waving of the hand about darkness and Gothic literature, and a reassurance that they are normal instrumentally rational people just like me and you (Hodkinson 2013; Spracklen and Spracklen 2012).

Goth subculture becomes as authentic as Disney-pink fairy fashions in the way other websites explain how to become a goth. For instance, just a few sites down on the first page of the Google search one can find a site called wikihow.com, which offers instructions on all sorts of things. One of these is on how to be a goth. It says (http://www.wikihow.com/Be-Goth, accessed 4 February 2014):

> Wear black. While there's a great variety of wiggle room in crafting a gothic look, almost all goth styles feature black or otherwise dark clothes. Dark purples and blues are also common as accent colors, but in general you'll want to dwell within the realm of darkness.

This is funny as a parody, but the website is perfectly earnest in its advice. The original post-punk and goth scene was not fixated on the colour black in clothing, and the 'realm of darkness' as an abstract piece of nonsense taken from a Dracula film. Black has become the colour of goth, but it is also the colour of most alternative subcultural fashions (and part of the common culture of the hegemonic culture), from punks to emos and metallers (this at least the Wikipedia site has got right). There is nothing uniquely goth about this, and nothing intrinsically dangerous any more about a look that is all about spending money to fit in with a whole bunch of other people. Commodification of alternativism (and commodification of alternative gender identities) has made it merely a fetishized lifestyle choice (Spracklen, Richter, and Spracklen 2013; Spracklen and Spracklen 2014). That is, people buy their alternative identities through the wearing of ready-made uniforms, not through close reading of politics. The page on being goth on wikihow.com continues by saying:

Fill your room or your basement with sensuous surroundings: think gothic in terms of light, color, and sound. Put posters on the walls of your favorite bands and hand [*sic*] dark draperies on the walls to soundproof your space, so you can play your music as loud as you want without disturbing the rest of your family. Creating a space for yourself will put you in a headspace where you're better shielded from the negativity of others. Since many goths are artists, writers, or musicians, it will also help you tap into the creativity and individuality that is such a big part of the subculture.

This is rebellion and alternativism at its most conservative – the one thing young people have to annoy their parents is loud music, but here, the evidently young would-be goths are actually dissuaded from doing something truly rebellious (Hebdige 1979). It is conservative in another way, too. It makes a big claim for goths being individuals by being like every other goth. In other words, the individuality is actually conformity and socialization into a social space, where everybody claims to be an individual, by 'thinking' gothic.

At goth.net, one of the most popular goth forums online, there are FAQs about goths that try to counter the stereotypes that are associated with the goth subculture among the mainstream. The writers of these parts of the website are carefully trying to dissuade people from becoming obsessed about rule books of goth and shades of gothness. In the section answering the question 'Am I a Goth?' the website answers (http://www.goth.net/faq/faq05.html#052, accessed 15 January 2014):

Generally if you wear and/or [*sic*] the exterior trappings that go with the subculture, and your musical interests reflect bands that are recognised within the scene and you feel at home within the scene and with it's [*sic*] members and their views and outlooks on life, you might possibly be Gothic. Please don't get obsessed by fitting the label, truth be told that many people who are Goth or who associate themselves with the scene don't call themselves Goths because they find it too limiting or find that others stereotype them based on that one label, rather than seeing the sum of the parts. Too often there are people that try too hard to fit the label and completely pass by the fact that being Goth is as much about being yourself and finding your own path rather than rigidly trying to fit the stereotypes.

The writers are correct to say people should not get too worked up over the label. But at stake here is an ideology of goth that is devoid of its radical, alternative ideology. Instead, there is only a shallow individualism that one finds everywhere in neo-liberalism as a form of instrumental conformity and hegemonic control (every dollar spent on leisure and culture is a dollar spent conforming to the modern ritual of individuality; Bramham 2006; Rojek 2010; Spracklen 2009): 'finding your own path'. Alongside that there is the reassurance that all you have to do to be 'possibly' goth is wear the clothes and embrace the look, like some goth bands on Facebook and share the 'outlooks on life' of goth's members. Those 'outlooks on life' are essentially extensions of the neo-liberal individualism at work: be yourself, buy yourself a niche that says you are different from everyone else beyond goth, consume and dress and think like everyone else within goth. This is bourgeois cultural capital at work (Bourdieu 1984): goth is just another way to purchase distinction and acceptability, and 'darkness' has just become another marketing niche selling clothes (and other products) that might shock a fundamentalist Christian, but are perfectly acceptable to wear to grandma's house at Christmas.

On the forums on goth.net there are many debates over the meaning of goth today, its sustainability as a subculture, and the differences between the goth subculture in the past with the goth scene of the current century. Most of the posters to the forums remain positive about goth's status as a viable subculture, and remain unflustered about the appropriation of goth by wider popular culture. However, there are dissenting voices. People are unhappy with the way the goth scene has lost its connection to the music, to alternativism as an ideology and radical politics, and to truly deviant or dark leisure activities and spaces (Rojek 2000). One discussion serves as an excellent representation of all these themes and issues. On 19 January 2014, Dieche started a discussion titled 'No one really makes a [*sic*] effort anymore' (http://www.goth.net/forums/viewtopic.php? f=17&t=16070, accessed 10 February 2014) [*all sic*]:

> For me it really feels like from the people I know no one in the Goth scene really makes a effort anymore unless its related to fashion or simply acquiring attention. I swear, any site you go on even Deathrock.com there's like no posts on people even trying to form a band even though the scene is supposedly music centered. Its kind of sad really, it just feels like everyone's so hollow. Yeah, sure, you dress nice but really? Whats the point of a pretty looking book if there's nothing worthwhile beyond that? Sure, 90's Goth bands weren't perfect but at least they 'tried'. Let me emphasize that a little more. 'TRIIIEEDDDD'. ... Yes, tried. Everyone now is always so catty and stuck up for no reason. I mean, seriously, if you had a reason to be cocky and stuck up then it would be a little more understandable but if you're some DJ that hosts some night no ones even really heard of or some random alternative model that does nothing more for the scene then just make it look like a superficial waste of time then yeah, that would be alright, but most people tend to be the latter. What happened to when it was more of a community and people didn't really care how freaking 'Gawf' you were and just liked the fact that you were even interested in the music? I'm fairly young so I wouldn't know too much about it but I always hear about the odd occasion when people actually bring it up.

Although written in non-standard English, the sentiment and argument can be discerned. The poster is angry that goth has become reduced to a fixed set of fashions and a fixed set of opinions about individualism, rather than a radical musical subculture. The poster is unhappy that goth music, the original driving force for goth and the way in which alternativeness and communicative leisure grew in the scene, has become unimportant to a superficial subculture interested only in rules of belonging. The only 'alternative' in this subculture is the 'random alternative model', the tattooed and pierced young woman who supposedly challenges patriarchy and the gender order by taking her clothes off (Holland 2004). For this poster, the meaning of goth, its communicative nature and its alternative ideology has become replaced by superficiality and the instrumental rationality of promoting women's bodies, goth nights and fashions.

A couple of the people who respond to the post are sympathetic, but for most of the eight people responding to date, there is strong disagreement with the sentiment and the argument. Goth for these respondents is about individualism and being dark and expressing that through fashions and lifestyles, and it is not tied to the music:

> You won't ever find me spending time trying to form a band, because I am a very busy man who can barely find the time and motivation for his writing. We all have different hobbies and things we do when work, household matters, time with significant others, errands, and so on are complete but there comes a point in life where that time is precious. (Oidhche-Yorath, posted 19 January 2014)

> I rarely attend goth clubs or try to meet up with other local goths (not that I'd know how though I'm sure there are local forums or something... I don't even care to know really at this point in my life). I have my education (getting my bachelor's in March) to focus on, my kids to worry about, and a new life in front of me at the moment. The last thing on mind is making an effort to be MORE of something that I already am. For me, I guess that's the equivalent of trying to be more bisexual than I already am. It's a part of me, sure, but I don't

have to show it off every chance to prove that to myself or to others. (Midieval Fantasy, posted 22 January 2014)

In this twenty-first century version of goth, the prevailing sentiments are that goth music and lived subcultures (clubs, scenes) are not as important as other things in busy lives. Being goth is merely a performance of alternative identity within the narrow limits of capitalism and hegemony. Being a goth is a form of alternative identity acceptable to capital, and acceptable to power. For Oidhche-Yorath, being goth means being a writer, and even the writing comes second to work and family. For Medieval Fantasy, goth is conflated with her celebration and virtual performance of her bisexuality – something to be mentioned while not really mentioning it, a carefully considered performativity of individual lifestyle choice and lifestyle consumption.

Extreme metal in the 1980s and 1990s

Heavy metal was an established part of the rock music scene in the USA and Europe (and many other regions) by the beginning of the 1980s. Bands such as Iron Maiden and Judas Priest were signed to major labels and made enormous profits from stadium tours and best-selling albums. Despite the importance of heavy metal bands to the wider music industry, heavy metal fans were often mocked or stereotyped as young, insecure, working-class white men (Walser 1993). For punks and those on the indie scenes, heavy metal fans and bands were scorned for their lack of radical politics, or for their conservative politics (Bennett 2000; Hebdige 1979). In the mainstream public sphere, heavy metal was marginal music, loud and simple (Walser 1993; Weinstein 2000).

Within the heavy metal scene in the 1980s, there was a proliferation of harder, faster sub-genres. Thrash metal became the popular sound of authenticity in heavy metal, metal played fast for true metal-heads to bang their heads to. As some bands moderated their music and lyrics to court chart success, younger metal musicians were determined to demonstrate their music was not soft, not mainstream, not poppie in sound (see demarcations in Weinstein 2000, 45–52). Keyboards were scorned in favour of galloping riffs. Vocal styles became harsher. Lyrical content and cover images became darker, playing with violence and Satanism. The underground metal scene thrived in the early and mid-1980s on the back of fanzines and tape-trading networks. Young metal fans buying magazines to read about Iron Maiden or Metallica could find adverts in the back of these magazines for fanzines and tape-trading pen pals. In this way, a whole extreme metal subculture emerged, governed by the rules of authenticity – what it means to be a true metal fan, or a true metal band (Kahn-Harris 2007). Nightclubs with metal evenings would play these underground extreme metal songs in their small rooms, or at unpopular times in between the mainstream metal.

Thrash metal continued to play a key role in heavy metal, but thrash bands such as Metallica and Slayer came to be over taken in the extremity stakes by bands playing what came to be called death metal. This form of heavy metal used blastbeats, a form of fast and heavy drumming, along with down-tuned guitars and 'cookie monster' growls for vocals. Extreme metal bands and fans started to label themselves with the 'death' epithet, and fanzines promoted a death metal ideology that embraced anti-commercialism from punk and hardcore, and anti-pop and anti-authoritarianism from metal (Kahn-Harris 2007; Spracklen 2006). Death metal then became commercially successful and popular in the mainstream of metal, following the cycle that thrash had followed. Almost immediately, some bands and fans rejected the death metal 'overground' and retreated into a

12

supposedly 'true' Satanism, more shrieked vocals alongside growls, and an adoption of strict ideas about fashion, musical structures and elitist (Satanic, nationalist) ideology (Spracklen 2006, 2013). This was the black metal subculture, which borrowed a term that had already been floating around on the extreme metal underground, but which they used (after some hesitation) at the start of the 1990s to identify themselves as a new 'true' elite (Kahn-Harris, 2007). Oslo, in Norway, became the focus of a number of bands and fans that started to change black metal's ideology and style, while spreading both across the underground.

Black metal existed in the extreme metal underground, spread and sustained by the same networks of fanzines and tape-traders that had sustained death metal. It might have remained an unknown and obscure subculture, but as it transpired, some of those musicians in Norway were determined to achieve some form of fame and notoriety (Kahn-Harris 2007; Spracklen 2006, 2013). The church burnings and murders associated with the second generation Norwegian black metal bands such as Mayhem, Burzum and Emperor gave black metal a global platform. Journalists and editors wrote stories about Norwegian black metal, metal labels signed black metal bands, and metal fans rushed to buy black metal albums and T-shirts. Musicians and bands changed their styles from thrash or death metal to black metal – Darkthrone from Norway being one obvious example. Black metal, however, carried with it unpleasant overtones of fascism, racism and nationalism (all of which coalesced in the bizarre writings of Burzum's Varg Vikernes; Spracklen 2006), so although black metal bands found audiences and fans around the world, they did not get signed to major labels or get into mainstream metal/rock magazines (unless it was in the news sections reporting on the latest court trials). Throughout the 1990s, then, black metal as a metal music space was globalized, but communicative and non-instrumental – black metal attracted scorn in the mainstream, and black metal fans and bands were marginalized, despite their importance and size in the wider extreme metal scene (Kahn-Harris 2007). Playing and listening to black metal were signs of resistance and alternativeness, even though the ideologies associated with it were elitist – and even though the bands were part of the commercial metal scene of labels, tours and management agencies (Spracklen 2006).

Extreme metal in the 2000s and 2010s

On first inspection, black metal continues to blaze in its northern sky. There are hundreds of bands and websites dedicated to black metal. There is a global scene of musicians, fans, independent labels and fanzines/blogs/sites that have sustained black metal. Some bands such as Watain have achieved commercial success and are signed to bigger labels, with global fanbases and crossover potential into mainstream metal. On Wikipedia, there is an extensive and mainly accurate account of the history of black metal and its continual evolution (http://en.wikipedia.org/wiki/Black_metal, accessed 31 January 2014; see also Spracklen 2006, 2013). This notes correctly that contemporary black metal bands are divided between those that claim black metal is about sticking to the stylistic, musical and ideological rules of the Norwegian second wave (ideologies of anti-Christianity, anti-modernity, nationalism; for styles see Kahn-Harris 2007), and those that claim black metal is a feeling or ideology of hatred and elitism that can be expressed through more experimental or progressive sounds. The key bands of the Norwegian second wave are good examples of this tension – as I have noted elsewhere (Spracklen 2012) – with some remaining true to black metal's sound (Immortal), and others retreating into primitive extreme metal (Darkthrone) or moving towards prog rock (Enslaved).

However, black metal as a subculture is at risk of being swamped by two different trends. The first is associated with the commodification of heavy metal more generally, and the loss of a distinct black metal ideology of elitism beneath the tide of commercialization. The second is the 'heat death' of the scene and the ways in which it has splintered and has been co-opted by hipster scenesters and musicians drawn to the thrill of murder and violence. Some websites and labels have disappeared altogether. At the same time, there has been an upsurge in commercial success for the older bands and some new bands that have been managed successfully. Larger black metal bands have become part of the lucrative festival circuits, headlining metal festivals around the world and earning enough money to not bother touring in the winter. This makes commercial sense, but does not support the sustainability of the live scene: smaller black metal bands struggle to play gigs in many cities and countries, where the extreme metal scenes have become dominated by newer genres of extreme metal and hardcore (Riches, Lashua, and Spracklen 2014).

Where black metal is still discussed online it is in sub-pages of larger metal fan forums. Black metal is thus presented as just one form of heavy metal, among all the other forms, for metal fans to choose to consume. As with the goth subculture, the fans online are generally enthusiastically supportive of their music and their subculture. Most conversations revolve around recommending bands and albums to each other, or promoting a new band from some obscure part of the world. There is clear evidence that black metal has globalized and attracts debate. But at the same time there is recognition that black metal has lost its elitist ideology and its ability to shock. Black metal is reduced to a simple notion of individualism, just like goth, a neo-liberal lifestyle choice that people can purchase (though that individualism has its limits on expressions of sexuality – see Spracklen 2010). One discussion on metalstorm.net stands as our exemplar in this section. On 9 February 2014, a poster called Karlabos (not this researcher!) started a discussion asking 'What is Black Metal nowadays?' (http://www.metalstorm.net/forum/topic.php?topic_id=49137, accessed 20 February 2014) [all sic]:

> And nowadays if you allow yourself to the black subgenres, you will see that most bands don't have the satanic imagery anymore, neither the lyrics are aimed to that concept. Also there are bands which have such a unique style that they went far from what one would consider a black metal band of the second wave. So … What is sufficient to categorize a band as 'Black Metal' nowadays?

The first person to respond showed how far black metal has evolved and changed, when they said 'I, for one, am super happy with the way black metal turned out, with branching out with subgenre after unique subgenre and, for the most part, abandoning that Satanic image (thank god)' (Lit.). Most of the other posters were also happy that black metal had changed from being elitist and Satanic to being something superficially 'individualistic'. One poster even argued that the Norwegian second wave was 'more or less afterthoughts in terms of influences [on modern black metal] and definitely aren't copied directly' (Troy Killjoy). This diminishing of the elitist, communicative leisure space of the 1990s black metal scene is not just bad history and re-writing of history; it demonstrates the way in which modern black metal fans (and musicians) have taken the danger and fire from the scene. Instead of burning churches[1] and raging against modernity, these fans prefer to spend their money buying vinyl releases of bands that take the eerie sounds of black metal without the lyrical content.

There is one dissenter in the conversation. Rasputin writes on 12 February 2014:

BM is a generational thing of an age where you traded tapes, where a PC was still on the horizon and not a part of everyday life, of a time where Underground could truly be called that, a time when Xtianity held its sway over most things, and people were scared of 'Satan,' now, all those things are gone. I mean, the changes are drastic, just think about what a horror film was back then, and what it is now ... That is why I keep saying and asking where is the relevance of this music today, or for that matter any Metal 'genre?' It is not there. Look at the American scene, it is filled with people who don't want to play their instruments and want to reduce their music to 'low brow' mentality of getting drunk as a skunk or getting high or getting into fights. If there was any wisdom, any intelligence or reason in our music, it is surely gone now. The same goes for BM, what once was is gone, and to try and perpetuate the same old thing is not only counterproductive, but it is extremely stupid ... I will be laughing 20 years from now, when I still see people in corpsepaint and shit, trying to make it 'KVLT' and 'real.'(...) The more stupid shit I see, the more I want to cut my hair, because I am becoming ashamed of the music I once was proud of representing, and that is not good.

So there are some musicians and fans who are still trying to centralize a communicative discourse about the meaning of black metal around radical resistance. There are still some who fight Christianity and modernity, who engage in communicative acts that try to keep radicalism central to the scene (Spracklen 2006). But these are already marginalized. The biggest change in the black metal subculture's communicative space has come from the co-option of black metal by hipsters (see discussion of the hipster in Schiermer 2009). Trendy, white, urban, middle-class people (typically men) have taken to black metal because of the scene's dark history. These are not the conservative, suburban middle-class men who became musicians in 1980s and 1990s Norway. They are urban, cosmopolitan omnivores. They are drawn to the danger and the reputation. But in becoming part of black metal they have tried to transform it in their own image. They have pushed to remove the elitist, Satanic ideologies and to replace them with positive messages of hope and belonging. Individual people can do what they like. But for middle-class hipsters with the right cultural capital, it is much easier to take control of a scene and change it in their image. Academics associated with the *Hideous Gnosis* journal have embraced published analyses of black metal that strip it of its original anti-authoritarianism and replace it with a mish-mash of individualistic impulses, ironies and transformative states of being. Black metal is reduced to ritual and transcendence. Black metal musician Hunter Hunt-Hendrix of the band Liturgy even managed to get a paper published in the journal where he writes (Hunt-Hendrix 2010, 61–62):

Transcendental Black Metal is in fact nihilism, however it is a double nihilism and a final nihilism, a once and for all negation of the entire series of negations. With this final 'No' we arrive a sort of vertiginous Affirmation, an Affirmation that is white-knuckled, terrified, unsentimental, and courageous ... The sun mesmerizes and burns. We participate in intensity because we are not sentimental and we know that death comes. But why not follow a goal, follow the sun and chase after its flairs? Why not go up in flames rather than dwindle to a speck of sand? The sun represents Truth and reveals all that it touches. We are honest because we refuse to lurk in the shadows, we refuse to point fingers, we refuse to perform our rites in secret. We are not sickly, spiteful, hateful. We do not hide behind costumes or esoterica.

Behind the incoherence and pseudish sub-cultural studies writing, there is a real problem. With their control of the knowledge-making apparatus, combined with bourgeois confidence and wealth that covers a lack of talent and intelligence, hipster versions of black metal (and post-black metal) seem to mark the end of black metal as a vital, communicative force against modernity and against authority. If we follow Hunt-Hendrix, we should all just be thankful that we are alive and stop being angry about things we cannot control. Black metal has been co-opted by the ruling elites and become an interesting plaything to amuse them.

Conclusion

There is no doubt that individuals within both subcultures, at the time of their specific emergence, refused to be radical, or pretended to be radical, or followed fashions and engaged in fights against outsiders and newcomers over who belonged. But there is also no doubt that the subcultures as they first existed were sites for communicative leisure and radical, alternative ideology. Goths and extreme/black metallers would probably argue that their subcultures are still thriving as communicative leisure spaces. These subcultures still exist in places across the world. They would say they are alternative by definition, by the choices they make around aesthetics, fashions, philosophies and music. I do not doubt that there are communicative moments in these scenes. I am sure that alternativism as radical oppositionality survives in some spaces and places, especially in countries and regions where there are real risks to one's life for choosing to be a goth or an extreme metaller. There may be some spaces where communicative action is possible and is happening – there are new musical scenes and subcultures that are emergent in a Williamsian sense (so new they have yet to be recognized by academics), and these may yet have the potential to break the cycle of appropriation and marginalization described by Hebdige (1979).

But the alternative in goth and black metal alternative culture has entropied, and there is a loss of anger and radical ideology. There is a heat death of politics and action. The ideal of the alternative music scene as a communicative leisure space is not matched by the reality of the instrumentalization of contemporary leisure – the submergence of agency and freedom in leisure in the structures of capitalism and late modernity. Identity politics still privilege elites with cultural and economic capital, and marginalization and hegemony act to restrict the working classes and other excluded groups from making real choices in their leisure lives. Leisure lifestyles and alternative leisure and culture are thus reduced to neo-liberalistic market choices. Rather, there has been a slow metaphorically entropic shift in alternative music, from a shared subcultural and counter-cultural leisure space – a space of direct political activism where potentiality and autonomy were possible – into one part of a globalized entertainment industry that has colonized the Habermasian lifeworld of leisure. Goth and black metal offers safe roles to play and identities to consume. With this heat death, their communicative, radical potential is extinguished like the light and heat at the end of the universe. In its emerging role as one choice of individual identity inside the neo-liberal machine, alternativeness becomes a matter of clothes and bands and choices, but loses its struggle to fight the system. The spaces left for real alternative leisure and culture in popular music are, as a consequence, very small.

Note

1. Not something I endorse, but the sentiment behind the church burnings was something that made the Norwegian black metal scene a genuine counter culture.

References

Adorno, T., and M. Horkheimer. 1992. *Dialectic of Enlightenment*. London: Verso.
Bennett, A. 2000. *Popular Music and Youth Culture: Music, Identity and Place*. London: Macmillan.
Bennett, A. 2002. "Researching Youth Culture and Popular Music: A Methodological Critique." *British Journal of Sociology* 53 (3): 451–466. doi:10.1080/0007131022000000590.
Bennett, A. 2006. "Punk's Not Dead: The Continuing Significance of Punk Rock for an Older Generation of Fans." *Sociology* 40 (2): 219–235. doi:10.1177/0038038506062030.
Blackshaw, T. 2010. *Leisure*. London: Routledge.
Bourdieu, P. 1984. *Distinction*. London: Routledge.
Bramham, P. 2006. "Hard and Disappearing Work: Making Sense of the Leisure Project." *Leisure Studies* 25 (4): 379–390.
Brill, D. 2008. *Goth Culture: Gender, Sexuality and Style*. Oxford: Berg.
Debord, G. 1995. *The Society of the Spectacle*. London: Zone Books.
Dilley, R. E., and S. J. Scraton. 2010. "Women, Climbing and Serious Leisure." *Leisure Studies* 29 (2): 125–141. doi:10.1080/02614360903401927.
Fendt, L. S., and E. Wilson. 2012. "'I Just Push through the Barriers Because I Live for Surfing': How Women Negotiate Their Constraints to Surf Tourism." *Annals of Leisure Research* 15 (1): 4–18. doi:10.1080/11745398.2012.670960.
Garland, J. 2010. "'It's a Mosher Just Been Banged for No Reason': Assessing Targeted Violence against Goths and the Parameters of Hate Crime." *International Review of Victimology* 17 (2): 159–177. doi:10.1177/026975801001700202.
Gramsci, A. 1971. *Selections from Prison Notebooks*. London: Lawrence and Wishart.
Griffiths, R. 2010. "The Gothic Folk Devils Strike Back! Theorizing Folk Devil Reaction in the Post-Columbine Era." *Journal of youth studies* 13 (3): 403–422. doi:10.1080/13676260903448021.
Griggs, G. 2012. "Why Have Alternative Sports Grown in Popularity in the UK?" *Annals of Leisure Research* 15 (2): 180–187. doi:10.1080/11745398.2012.659718.
Habermas, J. 1984. *The Theory of Communicative Action, Volume One: Reason and the Rationalization of Society*. Cambridge: Polity.
Habermas, J. 1987. *The Theory of Communicative Action, Volume Two: The Critique of Functionalist Reason*. Cambridge: Polity.
Hebdige, D. 1979. *Subcultures: The Meaning of Style*. London: Routledge.
Hesmondhalgh, D. 2006. "Bourdieu, the Media and Cultural Production." *Media, Culture and Society* 28 (2): 211–231.
Hodkinson, P. 2002. *Goth: Identity, Style and Subculture*. Oxford: Berg.
Hodkinson, P. 2005. "'Insider Research' in the Study of Youth Cultures." *Journal of Youth Studies* 8 (2):131–149. doi:10.1080/13676260500149238.
Hodkinson, P. 2011. "Ageing in a Spectacular 'Youth Culture': Continuity, Change and Community amongst Older Goths." *The British Journal of Sociology* 62 (2): 262–282. doi:10.1111/j.1468-4446.2011.01364.x.
Hodkinson, P. 2013. "Family and Parenthood in an Ageing 'Youth' Culture: A Collective Embrace of Dominant Adulthood?" *Sociology* 47 (6): 1072–1087. doi:10.1177/0038038512454351.
Holland, S. 2004. *Alternative Femininities: Body, Age and Identity*. Oxford: Berg.
Hunt-Hendrix, H. 2010. "Transcendental Black Metal." *Hideous Gnosis: Black Metal Theory Symposium* 1: 53–65.
Kahn-Harris, K. 2007. *Extreme Metal*. Oxford: Berg.
Lashua, B., K. Spracklen, and S. Wagg. 2014. *Sounds and the City*. Basingstoke: Palgrave Macmillan.
Lefebvre, H. 1991. *Critique of Everyday Life*. London: Verso.
LeGreco, M., and S. Tracy. 2009. "Discourse Tracing as Qualitative Practice." *Qualitative Inquiry* 15 (9): 1516–1543. doi:10.1177/1077800409343064.

Lucas, C., M. Decks, and K. Spracklen. 2011. "Grim Up North: Northern England, Northern Europe and Black Metal." *Journal for Cultural Research* 15 (3): 279–295. doi:10.1080/14797585.2011.594585.

MacDuffie, A. 2011. "Victorian Thermodynamics and the Novel: Problems and Prospects." *Literature Compass* 8 (4): 206–213. doi:10.1111/j.1741-4113.2010.00775.x.

Maffesoli, M. 1996. *The Time of the Tribes: The Decline of Individualism in Mass Society.* London: Sage.

Martin, B. 2004. "… And You Voted For That Guy: 1980s Post-Punk and Oppositional Politics." *Journal of Popular Music Studies* 16 (2): 142–174. doi:10.1111/j.0022-4146.2004.00017.x.

Pavlidis, A. 2012. "From Riot Grrrls to Roller Derby? Exploring the Relations between Gender, Music and Sport." *Leisure Studies* 31 (2): 165–176. doi:10.1080/02614367.2011.623304.

Riches, G., B. Lashua, and K. Spracklen. 2014. "Female, Mosher, Transgressor: A 'Moshography' of Transgressive Practices within the Leeds Extreme Metal Scene." *IASPM@Journal* 4 (1): 87–100. doi:10.5429/2079-3871(2014)v4i1.7en.

Rojek, C. 1995. *Decentring Leisure.* London: Sage.

Rojek, C. 2000. *Leisure and Culture.* London: Sage.

Rojek, C. 2010. *The Labour of Leisure.* London: Sage.

Schiermer, B. 2009. "Fashion Victims: On the Individualising and De-individualising Powers of Fashion." *Fashion Theory* 14 (1): 41–62.

Smith, C., and M. N. Wise. 1989. *Energy and Empire: A Biographical Study of Lord Kelvin.* Cambridge: Cambridge University Press.

Spracklen, K. 2006. "Leisure, Consumption and a Blaze in the Northern Sky: Developing an Understanding of Leisure at the End of Modernity through the Habermasian Framework of Communicative and Instrumental Rationality." *World Leisure Journal* 48 (3): 33–44. doi:10.1080/04419057.2006.9674452.

Spracklen, K. 2009. *The Meaning and Purpose of Leisure.* Basingstoke: Palgrave Macmillan.

Spracklen, K. 2010. "Gorgoroth's Gaahl's Gay: Power, Gender and the Communicative Discourse of the Black Metal Scene." In *Heavy Fundametalisms: Music, Metal and Politics*, edited by R. Hill and K. Spracklen, 89–102. Oxford: ID Press.

Spracklen, K. 2011. *Constructing Leisure.* Basingstoke: Palgrave Macmillan.

Spracklen, K. 2012. "Too Old to Raise the Horns? Getting Older on the Metal Scene and the Politics of Intentionality: A Case Study of Second Generation Norwegian BM Bands." In *Heavy Metal Generations*, edited by A. Brown and K. Fellezs, 79–87. Oxford: ID Press.

Spracklen, K. 2013. "Nazi Punks Folk Off: Leisure, Nationalism, Cultural Identity and the Consumption of Metal and Folk Music." *Leisure Studies* 32 (4): 415–428. doi:10.1080/02614367.2012.674152.

Spracklen, K., C. Lucas, and M. Deeks. 2014. "The Construction of Heavy Metal Identity through Heritage Narratives: A Case Study of Extreme Metal Bands in the North of England." *Popular Music and Society* 37 (1): 48–64. doi:10.1080/03007766.2012.724605.

Spracklen, K., A. Richter, and B. Spracklen. 2013. "The Eventization of Leisure and the Strange Death of Alternative Leeds." *City* 17 (2): 164–178.

Spracklen, K., and B. Spracklen. 2012. "Pagans and Satan and Goths, Oh My: Dark Leisure as Communicative Agency and Communal Identity on the Fringes of the Modern Goth Scene." *World Leisure Journal* 54 (4): 350–362. doi:10.1080/04419057.2012.720585.

Spracklen, K., and B. Spracklen. 2014. "The Strange and Spooky Battle over Bats and Black Dresses: The Commodification of Whitby Goth Weekend and the Loss of a Subculture." *Tourist Studies* 14 (1): 86–102. doi:10.1177/1468797613511688.

Stebbins, R. A. 2011. "Leisure Studies: The Road Ahead." *World Leisure Journal* 53 (1): 3–10. doi:10.1080/04419057.2011.552197.

Wallis, R. J. 2013. *Shamans/neo-shamans: Ecstasies, Alternative Archaeologies and Contemporary Pagans.* Abingdon: Routledge.

Walser, R. 1993. *Running with Devil: Power, Gender and Madness in Heavy Metal Music.* Hanover: Wesleyan University Press.

Weinstein, D. 2000. *Heavy Metal: The Music and its Culture.* New York: Dacapo Press.

Whitworth, M. 1998. "Inspector Heat Inspected: The Secret Agent and the Meanings of Entropy." *The Review of English Studies* 49 (193): 40–59. doi:10.1093/res/49.193.40.

Williams, R. 1977. *Marxism in Literature.* Oxford: Oxford University Press.

Williams, R. 1981. *Culture.* London: Fontana.

The restaurateur as a sustainability pedagogue: the case of Stuart Gifford and Sarah's Sister's Sustainable Café

Freya Higgins-Desbiolles[a], Emily Moskwa[b] and Stuart Gifford[c]

[a]School of Management, University of South Australia, Adelaide, SA, Australia; [b]Centre for Regional Engagement, University of South Australia, Adelaide, SA, Australia; [c]Sarah's Sister's Sustainable Café and Urban Activist, Semaphore, Australia

With the popularity of celebrity chefs, television cooking shows, gastronomic holidays and food festivals, it is clear that people's engagement with food is developing into a significant social phenomena. People are searching for ways to secure sustainable and ethical foods and are open to learning new possibilities. This article provides a case study analysis of the work of Stuart Gifford, a long-term sustainability advocate, restaurateur and urban activist. Gifford currently is co-owner of Sarah's Sister's Sustainable Café. This restaurant features sustainability in the design principles and management of the enterprise. Gifford's commitment to sustainability advocacy and teaching permeates not only the business but is also a life commitment as he undertakes initiatives such as fostering an external eco-market, creating sustainability events associated with a major metropolitan festival, community activism and political advocacy. This article analyses the import of Gifford's efforts. Employing a qualitative research methodology, this article presents rich insights into the ways in which running a sustainable café can be read as a cultural pedagogy. Employing Giroux's theory of culture as pedagogy, Gifford's work through Sarah's Sister's is considered as an alternative cultural pedagogy intended to counter the destructive pedagogy of neoliberalism and its attendant cultural values.

Introduction

Cafés have been a place where new ideas and revolutions have started. (Stuart Gifford, personal communication, August 15, 2011)

Hospitality, leisure and tourism are often thought of as hedonistic, pleasurable pursuits and are seldom viewed as sites where resistance to neoliberal hegemony and visions of alternative lifeways can be explored and expressed. Critical leisure studies offer an exception to this and have allowed scholars the freedom to bring concerns with equity and justice into our discussions of how individuals and societies undertake their leisure pursuits. This special volume with its invitation to consider 'the role leisure may play in fostering the development of "alternative cultures" which showcase viable models of sustainable relations between work, leisure and environment' has offered an opportunity to share research on the way a sustainable café has become a tool for teaching alternative, more sustainable living. While food studies have a long engagement with environmental sustainability through studies of 'green restaurants', we offer a different focus here on how enjoyment of food can be used as a tool for dialogue and debate for how we might create more sustainable communities. This discussion is particularly situated in recent critiques of neoliberalism and the ways in which this impacts on environmentalism and environmental and social sustainability (e.g., Harvey 2005; McCarthy and Prudham 2004; Sklair 2002). As McCarthy and Prudham state, 'neoliberalism is the most powerful ideological and political project in global governance to arise in the wake of Keynesianism … yet connections between neoliberalism, environmental change, and environmental politics remain under-explored in critical scholarship' (2004, 275).

Since the 1970s, sustainability has become a key concern for societies around the globe as a result of awareness of significant environmental crises. With Brundtland Report's articulation of the concept of 'sustainable development' in 1987, all arenas of human endeavour have been forced to come to terms with this issue. This paradigm shift has meant that we must transform the way we use the natural environment as a resource for development to protect essential ecological processes and with a commitment to intergenerational equity (World Commission on Environment and Development 1987). These transformations have flowed through to hospitality studies and processes and have recently been the subject of research and analysis (e.g., Melissen 2013; O'Neill 2009; Ryan 2009). Perhaps most important is the slow food movement which has a threefold agenda: promoting taste education, defending biodiversity and supporting small-scale, sustainable, local economies worldwide (Slow Food n.d.). Concomitantly, there have been societal transformations that demonstrate people's engagement with food and food cultures is shifting. This is exemplified in the popularity of celebrity chefs such as Jamie Oliver, television cooking shows like Master Chef in Australia, and a proliferation of gastronomic holidays and food and wine festivals held around the globe. There is also a context of emerging food crises which are catalysts to a transformation in food cultures. For instance, a predicted collapse of global fisheries is forcing restaurateurs to seek seafood from sustainable fisheries and sparked initiatives like the Ocean Wise Program in Australia (Ryan 2009, 26). Industry associations have been formed in response to some of these pressures, including the Sustainable Restaurant Association of the UK, the Green Restaurant Association of the USA and the Green Table Association in Australia.

This article presents a case study analysis of Stuart Gifford as a 'sustainability pedagogue' who teaches sustainability through his sustainable café called Sarah's Sister's Sustainable Café. He has been involved in the restaurant industry for 35 years, enjoying wide recognition and inadvertently creating a point of difference which has ensured his success and independence. Gifford has also been an urban designer and advocate for decades; for instance, he was commissioned by Port Adelaide Enfield Council to develop a finely illustrated work envisioning Port Adelaide 'as it might be' at a time when its redevelopment was on the agenda (Gifford 1998, 6). These experiences made him attractive as a research subject for understanding sustainability pedagogy.

Gifford defines sustainability as a commitment: 'we value the future and our children's well-being' (personal communication, June 6, 2011). Gifford has 35 years of experience of running this café which has moved between a number of locations in the Adelaide area and evolved in its operations to arrive at its current iteration in the seaside suburb of Semaphore. Gifford situates his vision of this café within the new area of 'urban ecotourism' where local enjoyment of the vitality of urban areas invites visitors to join in a convivial, creative and sustainable engagement with place. This phenomenon fosters an engaged and thriving community, enjoying consumption which has lower resource impacts, generates employment and fosters well-being and connectedness.

This research contributes to the area of critical tourism and hospitality studies. This new area of research is concerned with social justice and seeks to empower communities for more sustainable futures (Kincheloe and McLaren 2005). To date, no studies of the cultural pedagogy practised by restaurants have been made despite the fact that in public culture, the popularity of cooking shows and food culture demonstrates the area is ripe for study. This research uses Giroux's (2004) conceptualisation of alternative cultural pedagogy to analyse how sustainable restaurants teach clients alternative values.

Literature review

The topic of food and wine experiences in hospitality and tourism is of growing interest and increasingly subject to research. Engagement with sustainability has become an emerging trend in this area; for instance, chef Simon Beaton predicted the next big food service trend that would feature 'sustainable and responsible local practices focusing on green restaurants' (Beaton 2009, 8). However, perhaps the most exciting and innovative analyses have focused on the sociological implications of emerging food cultures and have employed innovative and trans-disciplinary theories.

Mak, Lumbers, and Eves (2012) applied world culture theory to analyse the impact of globalization on food consumption in tourism. They argued that, as glocalisation theory suggests, rather than forcing homogenisation of food consumption, globalisation may simultaneously act as an impetus to revive or even reconstruct local food traditions. This analysis demonstrates that social and cultural theories applied to food cultures yield valuable insights into the dynamics of transformations under way.

Peace (2008) provided an anthropological reading of the Terra Madre gatherings, the slow food movement's biannual gathering in Turin, Italy, depicting Terra Madre and slow food as a neo-tribal, postmodern movement challenging 'negative globalization' to promote a 'virtuous globalization'. Peace asserted that the slow food movement 'strives to establish a critical analysis of the power exercised by global forces over the local production and consumption of food, and seriously asks what can be done in response' (2008, 39). While Peace argued the movement fetishizes community food systems and traditional ways, for our purposes, we see this interaction over food, its production and its enjoyment as a place of dialogue over how we are to live.

Mair, Sumner, and Rotteau (2008) discussed the 'politics of eating' through case study analyses of three recent movements: slow food, food justice and organic farming. These authors situated their discussion in terms of 'critically reflexive leisure', which they defined as 'politically oriented leisure where the central components of reflection, resistance, and the articulation of an alternative vision inform and are informed by the dimensions of pleasure, activism, and empowerment' (2008, 381). By using this approach, they argued that food practices can be understood as 'a motivator for civic engagement, a source of knowledge, and a catalyst for change' (2008, 399). This case study of Sarah's Sister's provides a reinforcing example of such food practices in action as the subsequent analysis will demonstrate.

The theory employed in this analysis is culture as pedagogy, as used in Henry Giroux's analysis. Giroux is one of the world's leading social critics and educational theorists, and his work has particularly focused on cultural pedagogies evident in the classroom (e.g., Giroux 2006c). Here we take his theory into a new context of cafés and restaurants where we argue that we can read the practices of food cultures as cultural pedagogy. This is not an overextension of Giroux's theory; he claimed 'culture plays a central role in producing narratives, metaphors, images and desiring maps that exercise a powerful pedagogical force over how people think about themselves and their relationship to others' (2004, 111–112).

Giroux noted the 'regulatory and emancipatory relationship between culture, power, and politics' and how culture 'operates both symbolically and institutionally as an educational, political, and economic force that can be used to both support and resist the assertion of power' (2004, 117). Contemporary cultural pedagogy enacted by neoliberal globalization asserts that there is no alternative to the wholesale marketization of society; as Giroux puts it, market rule is presented as 'common sense' or even a force of natural law (2004). However, the hegemony of neoliberalism is not secure and uncontested. 'Culture is a crucial terrain for theorizing and realizing the political as an articulation and intervention into the social, a space in which politics is pluralized, recognized as contingent, and open to many formations' (2004, 111). Giroux's advocacy of a critical cultural pedagogy is seeking emancipatory possibilities and supporting resistance to the dominant paradigm with the ultimate aim of supporting radical democracy and human survival (2006a, 64).

In the industry domain, restaurants have been used as teaching venues as evidenced, for instance, in the seminars sharing environmental initiatives undertaken by Ted's Montana Grill chain (Romeo 2008, 14) and recent nutrition education interventions undertaken by celebrity chef Jamie Oliver. However, what we are reporting here runs deeper; it is a cultural pedagogy interrogating our values and lifeways and exploring alternatives. It is more in line with the worldview of Carlo Petrini, founder of the slow food movement, who argued that we need to build a 'new paradigm of food … this is the great challenge of the future; a new food policy to safeguard the planet' (2009). While we might not think of food and food service as a site of pedagogy, we are reminded of Santich's claim that 'all food carries meaning, whether through symbolic association or through the way it is used to deliver a message' (1996, 194). Recently, Flowers and Swan (2012) observed that understandings of food as a space for informal learning and pedagogy had been neglected, and so they convened a special journal issue on this topic in the *Australian Journal of Adult Learning*. To date, however, studies of food pedagogies have focused mainly on critically reading the efforts behind building alternative food networks, fostering food literacies and reading food geographies. This article makes a unique contribution through an in-depth analysis of the efforts of a restaurateur as a cultural pedagogue, using his café to teach alternative values and lifeways.

Methodology

This article is derived from a research project designed to develop an exploratory case study analysis of the role restaurants can play in cultural pedagogy by teaching not only more sustainable ways of engaging with food but also alternative lifeways. In order to gain such insight, the research methodology had to allow in-depth dialogue covering not only environment-friendly restaurant actions but also aspects of life history and the ways in which such life contexts might influence sustainability activism. Knowing Stuart Gifford to be a sustainability advocate of considerable impact in the Adelaide community, the first author identified the research opportunity available and pursued it without funding support as a facet of her wider critical research agenda.

Such a unique project necessitated unusual research methodology. First, we decided to use a single case study approach rather than pursuing comparative or multiple case studies. This was vital for us to gain the depth of insight and context-rich knowledge that we desired on this topic. As case study expert Robert Yin has noted, a single case study approach can be appropriate in certain circumstances and rationales for its use include critical, unusual, common, revelatory or longitudinal cases (2014, 51). Our case study has elements of a revelatory case which is described by Yin as arising from a 'situation when a researcher has an opportunity to observe and analyze phenomenon previously inaccessible to social science inquiry' (2014, 52). In our research project, the lead researcher has built a long-term friendship with the restaurateur as a local resident and an activist in the community which has resulted in bonds of trust and a commitment to longitudinal work together to use research as a tool for unpacking what his practice through the café has affected and means. Additionally, this case is arguably an unusual case as we have found few restaurateurs who have so strongly used their restaurants as a tool of pedagogy and community building in a way in which Gifford has. We derived inspiration for this research approach from Harris' (2009) work using a narrative approach to understand the supportive and familial working environment generated from the cultural values of a single hotel executive housekeeper – an exemplary model of single case study research. However, Gifford's interests, experiences and actions recounted in the introduction made him attractive not only as a research subject for understanding sustainability pedagogy but also as a co-researcher because of the rich understandings he has developed from his work and activism. Together we explored the vision, actions and impacts of the restaurant and evolved an understanding that resulted from a critical approach based on co-learning and action.

Accordingly, our research involved a series of semi-formal intensive interviews with Gifford in 2011 to understand how the restaurant is used to practise a cultural pedagogy of sustainability. These interviews were constructively built on each other and involved intensive dialogues to gain the deepest insights possible. In total, four interviews were conducted, each taking place at Sarah's Sister's. The interviews lasted between one-and-a-half and two hours each, and were tape-recorded and then transcribed in full.

Following transcription, the data were interpreted using a thematic analysis that comprised searching for emergent themes (Patton 2002; Veal 2006). This approach involved reducing the empirical material into categories guided by the interviewee's narrative without losing sight of the research aims (Miles and Huberman 1994). From these themes, insights and subsequent interpretations were made about the overarching role of the restaurant and the position of the interviewee as a sustainability advocate (Patton 2002).

Each transcript was originally subjected to interpretation at the ideographic level. Following this, the researchers searched for global themes as the four interviews were related to each other. This involved continually moving back and forth between each transcript's individual themes and the global themes that emerged, in a cyclical process containing different levels of interpretation (e.g., as recommended by Kvale 1983) ensuring themes were not too far removed from the interviewee's narrative (Thompson, Locander, and Pollio 1989). Further minimizing analyst bias, the interviewee also participated in transcript review after each interview. The opportunity was presented for him to clarify any statements he had made, and he was invited to contribute to the interpretation of themes.

Data from the interviews were supplemented by: participant observation at the restaurant during ordinary times and at certain special events; a study of the restaurant layout; and a study of relevant communications of the restaurant including publicity materials, the Facebook page and menus. This provided diverse and rich data to analyse, and the validity of the research was assured through analyst triangulation to minimize the effect of subjectivity (Miles and Huberman 1994).

Engaging Stuart Gifford as a co-researcher on the research project may cause some concern with a biased perspective. Such an approach is derived from a critical research methodology which acknowledges 'the meaning and significance of narrative work is co-constructed, involving the researcher, subject and reader' (Harris 2009, 151). While we acknowledge that this research, as a qualitative and interpretative work, may not conform to the conventions of positivist research traditions, we would argue that the richness of the emic perspective opened up justifies this approach. Related to this is the absence of anonymity in our reporting of the findings which is generally a convention in hospitality, leisure and tourism research. The purpose of this project is to share this as a model of practice, and so anonymity is anathema to our aims.

However, relying on one informant who is also a co-researcher in the project may potentially generate scepticism in our findings, so we sought multiple sources of corroboration of the assertions made in the interviews. External validation of Gifford's success is evident in the Australian Civic Trust award of 2007 which claimed:

> Stuart Gifford has driven his businesses with a strong focus on the environment and has used them to educate and enthuse the public ... [he] has set a standard that is an environmental and social model in business and the built environment. (Australian Civic Trust 2007, 8)

More recently, Sarah's Sister's was selected as a finalist in 2013 in the 'community' category in the Advertiser's Food Awards in which Sarah's Sister's was described as 'one eco-step ahead of the rest', named in the list of Adelaide's top 50 restaurants, and named in the list of the top 10 community restaurants (Mattsson 2013).

Sarah's Sister's Sustainable Café: overview of sustainability commitments

> As a major contributor to climate change, through high energy use and huge wastage, the hospitality industry's indifference and inaction is a disgrace. There is little triple-bottom-line thinking evident – Stuart Gifford, menu for Sarah's Sister's 2011.

The restaurant is located in the seaside suburb of Semaphore, in the capital city of Adelaide, South Australia. Semaphore is a short 20-minute drive north-west from the city centre, with the majority of its 100-plus restaurants, shops and businesses located along one main street leading to the beach. It has a very cohesive and engaged community, and despite experiencing large tourism growth in recent years as a destination in itself, it receives little state government support (S. Gifford [member of Semaphore Mainstreet Association Committee], personal communication, August 15, 2011).

Gifford calls his café an 'exemplar of life-cycle sustainability'. This begins with the choice of building and location for the current café. This café was opened in 2005 in a long disused butcher's shop built in the 1860s, which represents a reuse of a derelict building and thus entails little new resource use to construct. Gifford employed a number of passive design techniques which resulted in low-energy use in the operations of the café. The building had an extant brick wall interior which is used as a thermal mass heat trap that together with a north-facing building alignment allows good heating in winter which results in the need for little additional heating. For summers, which can be quite hot in Adelaide, cross-ventilation through the front door and an open back means little additional cooling is required; an evaporative unit is used only on the most extreme hot days. Additional techniques include: adjustable shade screens, over-design insulation, zonal control, skylights and energy-efficient lighting. Additionally, the café is co-located with the local garden centre, and the back of the premises adjoins the garden displays. This further cools the café in summer through the cooling effect of plants and the sprinkler system watering the plants (using recycled water). The fit out of the café and its kitchen features recycled furniture, and Gifford eschews the use of trendy kitchen appliances, employing a stove and mixer that have been kept going for decades with good care and commitment to repair.

Gifford started out with targets for 50% reductions in energy use and landfill which were easily exceeded. He found that within five years any costs of making the café run sustainably were met, and now the café runs on what he terms 'profitable sustainability' meaning savings represent profits for the enterprise. Together with the 'green marketing advantage' the café has as a 'sustainable café' he argues he has an 'unassailable business advantage'.

The menu is also a feature of sustainability. The café only offers vegetarian cuisine although this is not emphasized on the menu, in advertising, or in customer engagements. Gifford has been a vegetarian for decades for both ethical and sustainability motivations, as commercial meat production features intensive land use, environmental pollution and heavy water use (World Watch Institute 2004). The café also largely runs as a 'no menu' establishment, meaning the chef determines the food to be served. This reinforces the ability to serve local, in-season produce and reduces the typical wastage found in many cafés and restaurants. Gifford's priority has been sourcing local produce, with local food, beers and wines featured. This underpins the sustainability ethos of the café as local purchasing has community benefits and a reduced environmental footprint. While Gifford acknowledges that sourcing organic produce would also be highly desirable, he found that this was difficult to achieve from local suppliers, and so he decided local sourcing was his first priority.

Gifford is also creative in offering new experiences, events and activities. This commitment to creativity and innovation contributes to holistic sustainability in a number of ways. Gifford has instituted a weekly 'Parisian night' where Sarah's Sister's becomes a site of cultural creativity and conviviality. The creative food and wine offerings are enhanced by readings from a local poet and where clients are encouraged to open up discussions across the café. Sarah's Sister's has also hosted green wine events which have been used to inform clients about more sustainable and locally grown wines and to generate income for local vignerons. Additionally, Gifford has been involved with the Adelaide Fringe Festival, and, in 2011, Gifford hosted some of the events of the associated Future Food Festival at Sarah's Sister's to further his advocacy of sustainability through the restaurant (see below). With this brief overview of Gifford's practice as a sustainability pedagogue, we now present the results of the data analysis.

Themes and discussion

The interviews collected a range of data about Gifford's philosophy, practice and vision of running a sustainable café. They revealed his ongoing attempts to address the crucial pedagogical challenge of educating individuals and groups as social actors in the sustainability dialogue.

Sarah's Sister's as a model

Gifford views the example of Sarah's Sister's as a model for others. He interprets the narrative of his work as showing a movement from 'affordable sustainability' to 'profitable sustainability' (S. Gifford, personal communication, July 11, 2011). This articulation seems deceptively simple while it in fact contains profound insight. Gifford notes that sustainability is easily attained when you have abundant resources, but the trick for the small business owner is to identify what practices can be adopted at the outset that achieve sustainable outcomes at affordable and practical costs:

> The difference in our approach is the affordable approach. It's what we could afford in terms of developing a business ... if we had another [AUS]$100,000 then we could have had solar powered systems or a wind turbine, for the sake of a demonstration model, but we didn't have that budget. (personal communication, July 11, 2011)

Using the passive design techniques described earlier, resource and costs savings saw Sarah's Sister's transition from 'affordable sustainability' to 'profitable sustainability' smoothly and quickly:

> So in our case after about five years we've reached the breakeven point where we actually paid off all those extras it cost us to develop a sustainable business. So then after that you actually start making a profit out of it. You then become a lot more competitive than any other business. Because we're first, because we're so out in front, that advantage to us over other hospitality businesses is huge. (personal communication, July 11, 2011)

As a businessperson, Gifford also sees his model as underscoring the lesson that sustainability measures make sound business sense. This is in no small part also due to the fact that sustainability creates a business 'point of difference' and serves as a major marketing advantage (personal communication, June 6, 2011).

Participation in sustainability through consumption choices

On the menu, Gifford claims: 'by dining at Sarah's Sister's, your contribution [to sustainability] is *significant*!' However, Gifford also emphasized that his approach is a 'soft sell' making sure to not 'ram vegetarianism or sustainability down people's throats' (personal communication, July 11, 2011). There is a difficult balancing act of attracting the general public through a trendy and quality establishment while at the same time bringing them into a conversation about sustainable lifestyles:

> So if you can get them [the clients] to choose to go to a more aware restaurant, then it doesn't take very much to do it. If all the other things are as good as another restaurant, in terms of food, service and all those things, and then you've got this little edge, and if the people by the time they finish the meal they're aware of it, then you've got half a convert, and it hasn't been rammed down their throat, they've actually enjoyed the experience. (personal communication, July 11, 2011)

There is a clear difference between Gifford's advocacy as an activist and his pedagogy through the café, with the latter being subtle and letting the experience reach his mainstream clientele. This was clear in Gifford's discussion of his personal commitment to vegetarianism but his 'soft sell' of vegetarian cuisine through Sarah's Sister's:

Well there's not very many vegetarian restaurants and it almost went from there. From my point of view it's really important that it's a soft sell thing, it's friendly persuasion. I admire people who get out there and campaign and do all sorts of things ... [but here] people might actually end up coming just for the wines – they might come for the atmosphere, and then the vegetarian food was kind of irrelevant and we were converting huge numbers of people because they'd come and enjoy it. Quite a few of them would eat the meal, they wouldn't know it's vegetarian. (personal communication, July 11, 2011)

Gifford's activism works on several levels

Gifford's pedagogy occurs on a number of levels and with a range of intensity. On a daily basis, Gifford works for change through the practices of the restaurant as recounted in the section above on the restaurant design and operations. Gifford also hosts events for the community on a regular basis that are educational on the issues of sustainability that he supports. Additionally, Gifford has been involved with a major Adelaide festival, the Fringe Festival, and has in recent years hosted events at the café and supported other events which have been educative on food and sustainability issues. In particular, in 2011, Gifford was instrumental in the Future Food Festival, which was a sub-component of the Fringe. During this event, the café hosted a showing of the documentary 'Truck Farm', a 'Native Food day' and informational exhibits.

Gifford is also an urban activist in Adelaide and has participated in advocacy events like the major event in 2010 called From Plains to Plate. In 2011, Gifford was instrumental in creating an urban eco market for Port Adelaide which was an interesting blend of public information, ecological advocacy and green market generation. He has recently written policy documents on urban planning and transport issues for Adelaide and convened public meetings on local issues. However, the foundation on which Gifford bases his advocacy is his position as a long-term restaurateur. He views cafés as sites for exploring new ideas and planning revolutions, referring to the French experience. He has organized community events at his café and holds a vision of conversations between people creating communitas and engagement.

A vision for urban ecotourism

Gifford has a goal for the café to contribute to his vision for an innovative 'urban ecotourism'. Gifford believes that public policy should be focused on social well-being and community enjoyment of place, and that only tourism that enhances this and complements this should be supported and developed. This vision for urban ecotourism would encourage events, activities and developments which create a vibrant, creative and engaged space where tourists and locals mingle together and bring life to streetscapes previously dead afterhours. Gifford cites the Adelaide Fringe Festival's Garden of Unearthly Delights as a model of what can be done. This event, held since 2000, creates a temporary entertainment district in the the central business district (CBD) which creates vibrancy in Adelaide that is otherwise absent. It runs from midday to 1 am, attracting a diverse mix of people from the local population and visitors to enjoy risqué, cutting-edge and global entertainment; importantly, some of the programme is free of charge, and so people of all means can enjoy the conviviality of the Garden's space.

Discussion

Although Gifford's focus on a 'soft sell' of sustainable and ethical hospitality consumption could be criticized as a 'sell out', Gifford does communicate the more edgy topics in food consumption issues. For instance, his menu has a brief discussion of predicted impending food crises and food shortages. This is not the kind of dinner conversation one would expect in a hospitality establishment. His argument is that in sourcing food locally and having people engage with where their food is sourced, you contribute to an efficacious response to these problems.

Gifford says that the ordinary public can participate in sustainability by consuming at sustainable restaurants such as Sarah's Sister's. We need to critically read this assertion and challenge whether this ethical and sustainable consumption is likely to lead to the desired changes. Returning to Giroux's analyses of cultural politics and pedagogies, Giroux provided a critique of the marketing strategies employed by the clothing company Benetton in its 'United Colors of Benetton' campaign, which were provocative and allegedly engaged potential consumers in ethical reflections. However, Giroux's assertion was that the Benetton campaign in the final assessment meant 'social consciousness and activism in this worldview are about purchasing merchandise, not changing oppressive relations of power' (2006b, 71). For the cultural pedagogy of Sarah's Sister's to be effective in Giroux's terms, it has to go beyond mere consumption practices; if it remains merely communication of self and identity through consumption choices, it is sterile in terms of cultural change and in fact may only represent the market's takeover of cultural difference and relegate resistance to a market fad. Giroux urges us to 'recognize the political and pedagogical limits of consumerism ... individual and collective agency is about more than buying goods, and social life in its most principled forms points beyond the logic of the market as a guiding principle' (2006b, 86).

However, Gifford's efforts can alternatively be read as a creative resistance to the hegemony of neoliberalism with which Giroux is concerned. Giroux analyses the commodification of public spaces and the predominance of consumer values over citizen responsibilities and engagement in the market era of neoliberalism (2004). As Giroux exclaims: 'the good life ... "is construed in terms of our identities as consumers – we are what we buy"' (Bryman cited in Giroux 2004, 50). Gifford's work takes the commodified and privatized space of the café and recreates it as a public space to discuss citizen issues, recreate community and to educate on issues of the common good. Tellingly, people can attend events like the Future Food Festival events of 2011 without purchasing anything from the café. This can be seen as a way of countering the private sector's usurpation and commodification of public space; it is a creative use of the capacities for consumption to be educative, creative and building of holistic sustainability.

The work done through Sarah's Sister's is important because it is multi-fold. It holds educative events like the Future Food Festival, but Gifford noted that in many cases, this may be 'preaching to the converted' as already like-minded people are attracted (personal communication, August 15, 2011). This is why the subtle pedagogy of engaging ordinary consumers in sustainable consumption is very important. The café is reaching out to a wider populace with a 'soft sell', and they are open to it because it is enjoyable (personal communication, July 11, 2011). Sustainability is often mistakenly pushed on people in a negative fashion, fomenting guilt and implying that suffering is entailed. Gifford's pedagogy through the café emphasizes that sustainable approaches to food consumption are actually better and more enjoyable than the mainstream food industry. Gifford suggests that this can be segued into inviting customers into deeper and more complex

IMMEDIATE IMPACTS
The experience:
Surprise of no menu
Conviviality of the café
Virtuous consumption- participating in sustainability

The environmental goods:
Low energy use
Low waste
Recycled materials

Social goods:
Serves as a model others can emulate
Community embedded enterprise
Creates vibrancy on Semaphore High Street

Economic Goods:
Profitable sustainability model
Generates local employment and training
Generate local business opportunities (supply-chain, arts)

INDIRECT IMPACTS
Sparks new activities and models
Generates creative urban eco-tourism
Foments new awareness and consciousness
Contributes to required transitions

Figure 1. Conceptual model of Sarah's Sister's impact as sustainability advocate and model.

sustainability issues, as it opens up a space for dialogue and reflection (personal communication, June 6, 2011).

In terms of business sustainability, Gifford asserts that his practical sustainability efforts give him a green marketing edge. This assertion is supported by his café's profitability and bookings. It is also supported in the literature. Hsin-Hui, Parsa, and Self (2010) reported that consumers' awareness of a restaurant's green credentials was one of the important determinants of consumers' intentions to patronize a restaurant. The Sustainable Restaurant Association reported from a Populus survey that '70% of restaurant goers are more likely to eat in a restaurant recognized for its sustainability' (SRA n. d.).

Gifford's urban ecotourism fosters a synergy between the local's enjoyment of place with tourist visitation which presents a new way of seeing urban regeneration strategy and tourism development planning. Instead of fostering tourism plans which privilege high-end investment based on attracting the ever-elusive high-yield international tourist segments, his vision shifts the emphasis. He often refers to the example of the cosmopolitan city of Melbourne, Australia, where quirky developments, activities and events which appeal to the residents create a unique sense of place which then attracts visitors to enjoy this uniquely Melbourne space. The laneways of Melbourne featured in the state government's tourism campaign 'Lose Yourself in Melbourne' are an illustrative example of this. As a Melbourne promotional website states:

Often missed by tourists, Melbourne's laneways are a veritable treasure trove of bars, restaurants, galleries and boutiques. Melbourne's laneways are narrow enclaves where mainstream culture takes a back seat to allow for one-off boutiques, unique galleries, tiny cafés and hidden bars. (Only Melbourne n.d.)

Gifford's insights are generated by his unique life history where café ownership and urban activism enable him to think innovatively but based on practical experience. His recommendations feature the idealism of a visionary but the pragmatism of a long-term, small-business owner. The interviews also showed Gifford's energy for progressive social change. Through ethically inspired visions, he campaigns for enhanced links between education and social change. Sarah's Sister's Sustainable Café is the vehicle for communicating with the public and enabling the public to participate in sustainability. This leadership by a sustainability pedagogue is an important catalyst to transformation, and this study has exposed just how diverse the interventions can be from a singular source using a café as a base for action. We offer a conceptual model to outline the impacts of Sarah's Sister's Sustainable Café and Stuart Gifford's cultural pedagogy in Figure 1.

Conclusion

> You can begin an incredibly radical impact of international change by thinking about what you put in your mouth, by accounting and being accountable for what goes into your mouth and where it comes from. (Costa Georgiadis in Robson 2012, 30)

Critics of current practice under neoliberalism such as Henry Giroux (2004), David Harvey (2005) and Leslie Sklair (2002) have argued that we must resist the pressures of marketization and commodification under neoliberalism and identify alternative ways of living together sustainably. Gifford was selected as a case study of sustainability ambassadors using restaurants to practise a cultural pedagogy of alternative living. The plethora of sustainable and green hospitality establishments evident around the globe suggested to us that this was a worthy phenomenon for analysis. However, our research revealed that Gifford's efforts go much further than current 'greening' of the hospitality sector; his work entails a cultural pedagogy, exploring alternative ways of living and inviting his stakeholders into a conversation on the options available to us.

As research by O'Neill (2009) suggests, it is not easy for small hospitality businesses to introduce environmentally friendly initiatives due to their limited resources and a lack of support. However, Gifford models a different way of doing things where sustainability is a core value. For Gifford, business ownership and advocacy complement each other in synergistic ways, and he models a practice that might be transferable to other sites.

In his presentation to the Sydney International Food Festival in 2009, founder of the Slow Food movement Carlo Petrini exclaimed: 'I don't like to use the word consumers. We must become "co-producers". We are strong and we can bring change and if we all gather and collaborate we can really make this change'. Gifford's approach to using his café to engage café clients in sustainable food consumption through a 'soft sell' indirectly invites them into becoming such co-producers of change. However, for the practice to be instrumental in making substantial change in people's lifestyles, this gentle engagement needs to be a pathway to deeper engagement. Gifford's multiple levels of activities suggest that he focuses on more than just the ethical and green consumption offered by Sarah's Sister's. His current practice seems to embody what Mair et al. described in their food as politics argument: 'food, as intimate and vital, can be a motivator for civic engagement, a source of knowledge, and a catalyst for change' (2008, 399).

The case study illustrates the potential of restaurants as sites for practice of alternative cultural pedagogies and as advocates of holistic sustainability. It also offers a greater understanding of the complexities of sustainability and what role leisure, hospitality and tourism enterprises such as restaurants may play in promoting sustainable practice. It is clear from this research that such a simple, daily practice as eating can have revolutionary consequences if employed in a thoughtful practice of activism for transformation.

References

Australian Civic Trust. 2007. "Civic Review 2007." Awards Document.

Beaton, S. 2009. "Secret Ingredients." *Hospitality* 645: 8.

Flowers, R., and E. Swan. 2012. "Introduction: Why Food? Why Pedagogy? Why Adult Education?" *Australian Journal of Adult Learning* 52 (3): 419–433.

Gifford, S. C. 1998. *The Port: Heritage, Development and Prosperity.* Kent Town: Wakefield Press.

Giroux, H. A. 2004. *The Terror of Neoliberalism: Authoritarianism and the Eclipse of Democracy.* Boulder, CO: Paradigm.

Giroux, H. A. 2006a. "Border Pedagogy in the Age of Postmodernism." In *The Giroux Reader*, edited by H. A. Giroux and C. G. Robbins, 47–66. Boulder, CO: Paradigm.

Giroux, H. A. 2006b. "Consuming Social Change: The 'United Colors of Benetton.'" In *The Giroux Reader*, edited by H. A. Giroux and C. G. Robbins, 69–88. Boulder, CO: Paradigm.

Giroux, H. A. 2006c. *The Giroux Reader.* With C.G. Robbins. Boulder, CO: Paradigm.

Harris, C. 2009. "Building Self and Community: The Career Experiences of a Hotel Executive Housekeeper." *Tourist Studies* 9: 144–163. doi:10.1177/1468797609360598.

Harvey, D. 2005. *A Brief History of Neoliberalism.* Oxford: Oxford University Press.

Hsin-Hui, H., H. G. Parsa, and J. Self. 2010. "The Dynamics of Green Restaurant Patronage." *Cornell Hospitality Quarterly* 51 (3): 344–362. doi:10.1177/1938965510370564.

Kincheloe, J. L., and P. McLaren. 2005. "Rethinking Critical Theory and Qualitative Research." In *The Handbook of Qualitative Research*, edited by N. Denzin and S. Lincoln, 303–342. Thousand Oaks, CA: Sage.

Kvale, S. 1983. "The Qualitative Research Interview: A Phenomenological and a Hermeneutical Mode of Understanding." *Journal of Phenomenological Psychology* 14 (2): 171–196. doi:10.1163/156916283X00090.

Mair, H., J. Sumner, and L. Rotteau. 2008. "The Politics of Eating: Food Practices as Critically Reflexive Leisure." *Leisure/Loisir* 32 (2): 379–405. doi:10.1080/14927713.2008.9651415.

Mak, A. H. N., M. Lumbers, and A. Eves. 2012. "Globalisation and Food Consumption in Tourism." *Annals of Tourism Research* 39 (1): 171–196. doi:10.1016/j.annals.2011.05.010.

Mattsson, D. 2013. "South Australia's 50 Best Restaurants – Here Are the Finalists for the 2013 Advertiser Food Awards." *The Advertiser*, October 26. Accessed April 4, 2014. http://www.adelaidenow.com.au/lifestyle/best-south-australian-restaurants/story-fnizi7vf-1226746767586.

McCarthy, J., and S. Prudham. 2004. "Neoliberal Nature and the Nature of Neoliberalism." *Geoforum* 35: 275–283. doi:10.1016/j.geoforum.2003.07.003.

Melissen, F. 2013. "Sustainable Hospitality: A Meaningful Notion?" *Journal of Sustainable Tourism* 21 (6): 810–824. doi:10.1080/09669582.2012.737797.

Miles, M. B., and A. M. Huberman. 1994. *Qualitative Data Analysis: An Expanded Sourcebook.* Thousand Oaks, CA: Sage.

O'Neill, M. A. 2009. "Small Hospitality Business Involvement in Environmentally Friendly Initiatives." *Tourism and Hospitality: Planning and Development* 6 (3): 221–234. doi:10.1080/14790530903363407.

Only Melbourne. n.d. *Melbourne Laneways.* Accessed August 3, 2012. http://www.onlymelbourne.com.au/melbourne_details.php?id=9408.

Patton, M. Q. 2002. *Qualitative Research and Evaluation Methods.* Thousand Oaks, CA: Sage.

Peace, A. 2008. "Terra Madre 2006." *Gastronomica* 8 (2): 31–39. doi:10.1525/gfc.2008.8.2.31.

Petrini, C. 2009. *Presentation to the Sydney International Food Festival 2009*, October 18.

Robson, T. 2012. "Postcards from the Hedge." Interview of C. Georgiadis. *Wellbeing*, July 28–30.

Romeo, P. 2008. "Turner Evangelizes Earth-friendly Strategies along the Eastern Coast." *Nation's Restaurant News* 42 (16): 14.

Ryan, R. 2009. "Eye on Seafood Sustainability." *Hospitality* 653: 26–30.

Santich, B. 1996. *Looking for Flavour*. Adelaide: Wakefield Press.

Slow Food. n.d. *Slow Food*. Accessed October 8, 2012. http://www.slowfood.com/.

Sklair, L. 2002. *Globalisation, Capitalism and Its Alternatives*. Oxford: Oxford University Press.

Sustainable Restaurant Association. n.d. *Why join the SRA?* Accessed October 8, 2012. http://www.thesra.org/what-we-offer/membership/.

Thompson, C. J., W. B. Locander, and H. R. Pollio. 1989. "Putting Consumer Experience Back into Consumer Research: The Philosophy and Method of Existential-Phenomenology." *Journal of Consumer Research* 16 (2): 133–146. doi:10.1086/209203.

Veal, A. J. 2006. *Research Methods for Leisure and Tourism: A Practical Guide*. 3rd ed. Harlow: Pearson Education.

Yin, R. K. 2014. *Case Study Research: Design and Methods*. 5th ed. Thousand Oaks, CA: Sage.

World Commission on Environment and Development. 1987. *Our Common Future*. Oxford: Oxford University Press.

World Watch Institute. 2004. "Is Meat Sustainable?" *World Watch Magazine*, July/August, 17 (4). Accessed June 14, 2014. http://www.worldwatch.org/node/549.

Community-supported agriculture from the perspective of health and leisure

Bernadett Kis

Juhász Gyula Faculty of Education, Institute of Applied Health Sciences and Health Promotion, University of Szeged, Szeged, Hungary

Community-supported agriculture (CSA) is a rapidly growing movement responding to the global economic crisis. The concept of CSA is thought to have originated simultaneously in Japan and Europe in the 1960s and then spread throughout the USA. In its essence, a CSA involves a direct connection between a farmer and the people who share the risks and rewards of growing and distributing food. The benefits, according to widespread international research, are plentiful: economic, environmental and social. In Hungary, CSA is a relatively new idea and in the last few years there have been not more than five or six so-called share CSAs established, one in the author's hometown. The paper presents how the French variation of CSA (AMAP) was adopted in Szeged, Hungary and how this vegetable community works and what are some of its leisure and health impacts on the author. The paper also attempts to interpret the author's CSA membership from a health and leisure perspective connecting this idea to health promotion and to Blackshaw's 'liquid leisure' concept.

Spring

The idea for the study on which this paper is based emerged when I was looking at a photo taken at a farm event on a sunny Saturday morning in September 2012. Most men in the picture are collecting heavy pumpkins, while the women are busy cooking a large bowl of ratatouille. Some children are crawling on and into the boxes of pumpkins, others are trying to use the corn shredder. All seem to be enjoying what they are doing. One among them is me. Calling back my memories of that harvest feast, questions arose in me: what is happening there? What am I doing there? Am I working? Am I spending my leisure time? Or am I promoting my health? Or all of these?

Of course these questions did not come out of the blue. I am a psychologist working in higher education in an institute of health promotion and I have been a member of a community-supported agriculture (CSA) initiative for two years spending a lot of my leisure time in it. CSA is a particular approach to the production and distribution of local food. It is based on the direct connection between a nearby farmer and people who eat what the farmer has produced. An early proponent of the movement, Robyn Van En summed it up like this: 'food producers + food customers + annual commitment to one another = CSA + untold possibilities' (Henderson and Van En 2007, 3). The commitment

---

An earlier version of this paper was delivered at the Midterm Conference of the International Sociological Association Research Committee on Sociology of Leisure in Szeged, Hungary, 18–20 September 2013.

is advantageous for both sides; the farmer can build a direct and long-term relationship with his customers, paying attention primarily to food production, and the customers will know where the food comes from, how it is produced and who produces it (Réthy and Dezsény 2013). This notion of the farmer's accountability to the customers is largely responsible for the emergence of several local agricultural forms (e.g., farmers' markets, community gardens, direct marketing production; Mair, Sumner, and Rotteau 2008). The distinguishing feature of CSA is its capacity to establish communities around the interwoven issues of food, land and nature (Groh and McFadden 1997). People support local producers who respect the integrity of the ecosystems (Mair, Sumner, and Rotteau 2008), who know that the health of the ecosystems lies in diversity, connectivity and relationships which have been cut up by capitalism (Büscher et al. 2012). CSA belongs to those movements which seek to 'to de-link wholly or partially from the overwhelming powers of neoliberal globalization' (Harvey 2005, 200–201) and can be seen as a step towards the decommodification of food (Hinrichs 2000) and nature. It brings together producers and consumers in a local food network where the farmer engages in supplying the customers with whatever the farm gives throughout the year and the consumers' engagement is manifested by their upfront payment and commitment for the entire season. In this effort, consumers become 'sharers' of a farm (philosophically they have their common farm) and they share both the 'inherent risks and potential bounty' (Henderson and Van En 2007, 3). By changing both production and consumption patterns, CSA offers a partial alternative to the ruling economy. As CSAs have strong links to the organic farming movement which addresses sustainability questions, CSA is also seen as a solution to problems presented by modern industrial agriculture (Vadovics and Hayes 2007). The emergence of the French AMAP, the Portuguese Reciproco, the Canadian Agriculture soutenue par la communauté and many more CSAs worldwide show that people from different countries respond the same to the challenge of globalization and try to adapt CSA principles to local features (Henderson 2010).

In Hungary, the idea of CSAs is relatively new; besides an attempt of the Open Garden Foundation (Nyitott Kert Alapítvány) at around the millennium – when consumers after the restricted economy of the socialist regime seemed not yet ready for an economic model which offered limited choice (Vadovics and Hayes 2007) – there have not been such initiatives until a few years ago. Even now there are only half a dozen so-called share CSAs in Hungary, the creation of which was a result of a project coordinated by the international network of community-supported agriculture, URGENCI, to disseminate the French AMAP[1] concept in Central and Eastern Europe (Henderson 2010). One of these CSAs is the Wheel of the Year Ecofarm where I am a member and where the farmers wanted to establish a CSA like farm and community based on the French AMAP principles.[2] As they say their mission is to create 'a network connecting CONSCIOUS urban and rural people who are RESPONSIBLE for their own health and that of the environment, as well as INTERESTED in local communities and the landscape around them' (http://evkerek.blogspot.hu/).

So the roots of my original questions came partly from my involvement in this Vegetable Community and partly from my experience as a university teacher in an institute of health promotion. There was one more thing: our institute was to hold an international conference on leisure. It was then that I started focusing on leisure and wondering about my own leisure in the light of my CSA membership. Empowered by Blackshaw (2010, xv), who in his book, *Leisure*, 'rejects the pre-ordained distribution of academic territory which normally decides who is qualified to speak about what', I decided to investigate my membership from a health and leisure perspective, the former being a known, the latter being quite an unknown aspect for me. I just felt that a traditional, structuralist view on leisure, which I was familiar with, would be too narrow and outdated in the twenty-first century to describe my leisure associated with my CSA membership, so I wanted to explain and interpret it in the light of literature which demonstrate how leisure is reappraised in a postmodern context (Blackshaw 2010; Rojek 1995, 2001, 2010).

One may ask whether a CSA membership qualifies as a leisure activity. Here I rely on the arguments of Ravenscroft et al. (2013) who in making reference to Roberts (2011), Mair ([2002] 2003) and Blackshaw (2010) says 'yes'. So I decided to dedicate an entire season (from the spring of 2013 till February 2014) to observe, analyse, critically reflect upon and interpret CSA from the perspective of health/promotion and leisure. Deciding on an appropriate methodology was not an easy task. I knew that it would be impossible to distance myself from the material; I bring my background and my identity into this research, and this should be obvious. I took to heart Peshkin's discussion on the role of subjectivity:

> My subjectivity is *the* basis for the story that I am able to tell. [..] It makes me who I am as a person *and* as a researcher, equipping me with the perspectives and insights that shape all that I do as a researcher. (Glesne and Peshkin 1992, 104)

So subjectivity was something to capitalize on. I would position this paper on what Behar (1996, 174) calls the 'borderland between passion and intellect, analysis and subjectivity, ethnography and autobiography, art and life'. My study seeking to address the questions of what my CSA membership tells us in terms of health/promotion and leisure and how leisure, health and community-supported agriculture can be connected fits this concept as being on the 'borderland' of disciplines.

I applied the researcher as participant research methodology. My status was a complete member as I fully immersed in the research setting to 'grasp the complete depth of the subjectively lived experience' (Adler and Adler 1994, 380). Data were collected from participant observation, personal discussions, personal communication, farm news-letters and documents, the community mailing list and records of core group meetings. I also used my feelings and reflections from auto-observation as vital data for understanding the world of CSA. First my observations were more general and over time they became more focused. The data collection process was intertwined and interactive with data analysis and interpretation. I identified key themes in my field notes and looked for interconnectedness between leisure and health associated with CSA. The three themes are: pleasure connected to food and eating, resistance and gifting, and I added two from scholarly literature on postmodern leisure: devotional practice and search for meaning derived from liquid leisure (Blackshaw 2010) and civil labour (Rojek 2001, 2010). These five themes form the basis of my analysis and structure my narrative. This paper is both a process and a product. It tries grasp how I have changed throughout my study and how it has reorganized the work–leisure relationship in my life. The narration follows the changing of the seasons in deep honour of our farm, the Wheel of the Year Ecofarm.

This farm is a small, independent, labour-intensive certified organic family farm run by a young couple, who have qualifications in agriculture. They produce more than 100 different types of vegetables per year. Some of these are heirloom vegetables which are not used in modern large-scale agriculture. Their customers are called Members. The farm provides 40 boxes of vegetables a week, which practically means that they supply 60–65 families with vegetables week by week.

There is a written agreement between the farmers and each member of the community, signed before each season, in which mutual commitments are laid down. It specifies the time and place of the distribution of the boxes and the payment conditions; members are to pay monthly, which is not as strict as the French AMAP model in which customers are to pay for the whole year before the agricultural year begins. The farmers, as they say, would not have had the courage to ask for full prefinancing within Hungarian conditions. They try to increase gradually the length of the commitments to make people get accustomed to this new economic and social initiative. The agreement mentions and the farmers themselves keep on emphasizing that the money the customers pay is not for the price of the vegetables but financing of the production of the vegetables. Actually, the whole year budget of the farm (all costs and human work) is distributed among the community members. For some people, it might be difficult to adapt to the system at the beginning. However, the weekly farm newsletters, the exchange box at the pick-up point and the possibility of sharing the boxes serve to ease this adaptation.

The year 2013 means a change in the farmers' lives. Because of environmental and personal reasons they have decided to give up the Budapest community where they have also delivered their produce, so the Szeged community is to be enlarged. As the first rays of the sun come out, I get news from them on the community mailing list stating that a meeting is going to be held to recruit some new members. Old members are welcome to speak about their experiences. Though I have loads of work to do, I cannot resist going as I am deeply grateful for what we got last year from the farm and the community. I listen again to the accounts of the farmer's wife on the French AMAP and I am again (and ever since) fascinated by both the idea and her character. A young woman with calloused, workman's hands, full of enthusiasm, natural charm, and authentic and clear thoughts.

I look at the people and wonder why they are here, what motivates them to join a CSA. I recall my memories of my first encounter with the CSA. It was two years ago that with loosened familial ties, being a bit disillusioned by the structural transformation of the Hungarian higher education, I was looking for new impulses in my life and was on a quest to find a livable community when I saw the notice about a forthcoming meeting at the local Waldorf school about CSA. The scene attracted me as Waldorf pedagogy is characterized as 'alternative', so I assumed that this initiative was something considered alternative. One more thing that attracted me was that it was associated with food, healthy food, and as being passionate for gastronomy I was more than curious though I thought, as a health promoter, my husband and I were on a healthy diet.

This audience seems to grab the message of AMAP: the farm needs people, people need the farm. After the presentation, four of us are speaking about our experiences of the previous year. All of us mention that it is invaluable to have freshly harvested, seasonal organic produce every week from kind, authentic and deeply committed people who grow these vegetables with utmost care and love. We speak about how the system has changed our cooking and shopping habits, which seems to be a usual consequence of being a member according to most studies (Saltmarsh, Meldrum, and Longhurst 2011).

This time the introduction of the applicants is left out which I feel is a bit of a loss compared to last year when sitting in a circle we introduced ourselves and spoke about our motivations to join. I remember telling everyone that besides having local fresh food, I was looking for a community, which made me an odd-one out. The majority of the people expressed their wish to have an access to quality food and there were also some whose motivations went beyond it; these people wanted to support a local farmer and small-scale agriculture. Both motivations are characteristic of people applying for an AMAP membership (Girou 2008). The introduction seemed useful as it turned out that some of us live very close to each other, though we had never met before. The seeds of a community were sown there.

As the weather gets warmer, we are called to take part in a meeting at the farm to start the season. It is a good opportunity for us to learn more about the farm and farming techniques and mingle with the new members. The farm is marvellous, neatly arranged, we can find every shade of green. Beautiful beds abound, we are convinced that the vegetables are produced in an organic way. The stuffed socks we see inbetween the salad lines intrigue us, and we learn that they are filled with wool because it is said that wool keeps roes away. Knowing that our vegetables are produced in a sustainable and resilient way gives us a feeling of trust. I proudly watch this marvellous farm and the beautiful landscape and think that it exists partly because of my and the community's commitment to our CSA.

The season starts and the first pick-up day has arrived. I am eager to meet the community members again and to see what nature can offer us at this time of the year. The first box contains asparagus, chives with their edible flowers, sunchoke, arugula and many more marvellous vegetables. I cannot resist smelling and tasting them. During the evening, I am sitting in our garden with my husband with two plates of fresh green vegetables, a real treat for us, a gift from the farmers and nature. As the rich flavours of these vine-ripened vegetables are exploding on our taste buds, we feel that this is one of the biggest luxuries in this modern consumerist world. I think everyone should have the right to access such fresh and healthy food.

As we are well into May, I decide to build a composter because there is so much green waste from the vegetables, and I feel this is so precious, part of something that was grown with love and care, that we should give it back to the life cycle. It takes a day for us to plan and build the wooden composter but by the end of the day it stands in the corner of the garden and we proudly watch our creation. Recycling enlivens our home, new waste collection techniques are being formed. I really feel now that we contribute to the health of the environment. I do not just teach about environmental health at the university, but actively do for it. CSA slowly permeates my life.

Summer

The season of growth, bounty, pleasure and love. Boxes are filled with various kinds of salads, other leafy greens, carrots and fennel with its immensely mild long green edible leaves, rainbow coloured Swiss chard and courgettes in various shapes and colours, fragrant herbs which usually decorate and perfume our home until they are eaten.

During the summer pick-ups, after putting the vegetables into my basket, I often sit under the huge, shady trees and share ideas with other members about food, family, life or environmental problems or watch children playing and members coming and lining up at the registration table waiting their turn to tick their names. Most of them do not seem to be annoyed that the members at the beginning of the queue and the farmer get into lengthy conversations. The pace and time are slower in this food community. We seem to be part of a growing minority who chooses slowness over speed. The Slow Movement propagates the right to determine our tempos so to live and do things at the right speed. By doing this, we can reclaim 'the time and tranquility to make meaningful connections' (Honoré 2004, 277) with people, with nature and with ourselves. So this community is immune to the 'hurry virus', the feeling of having to rush all the time which has been identified as a cause of illnesses (Tranter 2010). This is certainly a health benefit and there are some more. With statements like 'I'm all green inside' or 'My body is purified and I have clearer thoughts', members express that eating these vegetables contributes to their physical and mental well-being and they also support the health of the environment. The idea of CSA encompasses all perspectives of a modern health conception: the physical, mental, social, environmental and the spiritual dimensions (Benkő 2005), and I have a deep conviction that what happens here is health promotion in action. The World Health Organisation's (1986) Ottawa Charter defines health promotion as 'the process of enabling people to increase control over, and to improve their health'.

But how is it possible that my discipline, health promotion has not embraced the notion of sustainability? The problem has several levels. First, people promoting sustainable agriculture are mainly environmentalists with a systems orientation, while health professionals are trained in one or two disciplines and as a consequence have narrower insights into the food theme. Second, the problems of industrial agriculture are not described in key health concerns and while a person can be aware of the challenges of the global food system, it is difficult to integrate it into the current health paradigm (Cohen et al. 2004).

Also after the millennium, the health promotion community addressed the new forces that shape our health: new patterns of consumption and communication, commercialization, global environmental change and urbanization. The answer from health promotion officials was the creation of the Bangkok charter (World Health Organisation 2005), in which one of the key commitments was the focus on communities and civil society saying that they 'often lead in initiating, shaping and undertaking health promotion. ... [E]mpowered communities are highly effective in determining their own health, and are capable of making governments ... accountable for the health consequences of their policies and practices'. In 2006, the Health in All Policies initiative was proposed during the Finnish presidency of the EU stating that health must become a critical goal of all governments.

Taking a look at these milestones of health promotion, I must say that the goals have been expressed but the implementation is still lagging behind. The civil society and communities, including the communities around CSAs, being conscious of these new forces that shape our health could react quicklier than governments. The initial role of these communities in promoting health is even more transparent when we learn that sustainable development and health promotion has not been linked for long. It was only in 2010 that Kickbusch linked the two agendas saying that 'in many cases, the best choices for health are also the best choices for the planet; and the most ethical and environmental choices are also good for health' (7). Recognizing the decisive role of the food system in what we eat and critising today's global food system as being dangerous to the health of the people and that of the environment, she urged to put food governance, production, distribution and consumption into the focus of health promotion. What she proposes to do at the global level, we do in our CSA at a local level. Soon I arrive at a whole-systems level of thinking: the importance of interconnectedness, relationships, consequences and feedback loops. I understand the disappointment of the elderberry producer who usually sells his products during the time of the pick-ups while he speaks about the efforts of local producers to sell their seasonal products in the shadow of big corporations.

As the food theme is a 'disciplinary buffet table' (Mair, Sumner, and Rotteau 2008, 381), it is not only health promotion that arrives at it but also a whole range of disciplines including leisure studies. The upcoming conference of the International Sociological Association Research Committee on Sociology of Leisure (Benkő, Tarkó, and Lippai 2013) organized by our institute gives me the opportunity to have a closer look at my CSA from the perspective of leisure and leisure studies. As a psychologist, I have just a strong intuition that my leisure can neither be described in terms of free time (De Grazia 1964, Lippai 2007) or activity (Kelly 1996), nor as a residual category of work (Slater 1998). There must be more to it.

My intellectual wanderings about leisure start with the Beijing Consensus on Leisure Civilization, a document of the International Sociological Association Research Committee on Sociology of Leisure (2010). I am deeply impressed by the wording and spent half a night trying to translate it to share with my collegues. It is so close to what I think of leisure. The parallel with health and health promotion seems evident for me. I find that the same forces have shaped our health and leisure, and the reaction from the leisure studies community and the health promotion community are very much alike. By making references to the respect of nature, reducing waste, promoting an environmentally friendly life, I feel sustainability is hidden among the lines, the very theme addressed by the health promotion agenda. In parallel with the spiritual dimension of health is the deep and creative contemplation that leads us to discover the true goal of life. Informed by Blackshaw (2010), I also find another parallel with health. As in modern health approaches, the focus is on how individual people interpret their health, what meaning they give to it, I feel the focus in leisure studies has moved towards the lived experiences, 'to place people's experience of leisure as the centre of their analyses' (115).

One of the key themes in our community is pleasure associated with food and eating. One source of pleasure comes from the sheer beauty of these vegetables. The experience can be compared to the aesthetic pleasure of watching a painting or other works of art. The other source of pleasure comes from the taste of these vine-ripened, chemical free products. A lot of members assert that they do not find any pleasure in eating store bought vegetables. Even their children turn away from these products. The pleasure of food and eating is also at the heart of the Slow Food Movement such as the propagation of eco-gastronomy, 'the notion that eating well ... should [,] go hand in hand with protecting the environment' (Honoré 2004, 58). The fusion of pleasure and ecological principles is the very theme our CSA is about. So to supplement what I have mentioned above: often the best food choices are the tastiest and healthiest; what is good to our health and the health of the planet is often the tastiest. By this emotional or sensual involvement, the preparation of food and eating becomes a leisurely activity and eating is not just a maintenance for life but enhancement.

Community festives and rituals are a good way to celebrate food and indulge in social relations. In August, there are some hints to me from the farmers to organize the bread feast but my other personal commitments sweep away even the idea of it in my mind though I am eager to feel what I felt at last year's bread feast. We were getting around a table under a huge shady tree and while sharing our home-made bread, pastes and marmelades, we were swapping ideas about food and life. It was a true convivial athmosphere. I remember telling the members that one thing that cannot be speeded up is bread baking. I use wild yeast which forces me to slow down and this adds a spiritual dimension to bread baking. This is my attempt to live better in a fast-paced postmodern world and I hope this act of deceleration 'gives another push to the Slow Movement' (Honoré 2004, 17). By changing how we think about food as one of our most basic needs which connects us to Mother Nature, we are changing our lifestyle (Benkő et al. 2009). I agree with Alice Waters, Slow Food International governor, that 'Loving food is the most personal and least abstract way to be an environmentalist'. So while eating can be a leisurely activity which is connected to pleasure, it is also a health issue, and 'an agricultural act' (Berry 1990, 145).

Autumn

As August gives way to September, the leaves on the trees begin to change, for a transitory period the farm still gives us the bounty of heirloom tomatoes with the flavour of summer, but at the same time root and tuber vegetables appear in our boxes that are much more characteristic of autumn. On the first pick-up day of September agreements for the autumn–winter are to be signed by both the farmer and the member. I notice a nice and friendly handshake between a member and the farmer, a gesture which I have never seen before. As I overhear their conversation, they are shaking hands for the fruitful partnership and the farmer is thankful for the trust and support. This handshake can be a symbol of a local food sytem but not that of the global food system. According to Anderson and Cook (2000), a local food system 'reworks power and knowledge relationships' (112) by restoring the distorted physical, social and metaphysical distance between farmers and consumers and 'gives priority to local and environmental integrity before corporate profit-making' (112). I become more and more aware that the involvement in our CSA has political implications related to power and ideology. There are a lot of statements within the community which uncover the resistance to the dominant food system. People often express their opposition to giant corporations and the agribusiness food complex. Members admit sometimes being ashamed that they do their weekly shopping in one of the supermarket chains even though they know they should refrain from it, as if it were a central value of this culture-sharing group to resist these temples of consumerist culture. Soon I also discover my own resistance through disagreements with my husband about where to shop and through the suspicion with which I search for the origin of a product. In our CSA, there is no need to look for labels, detecting the source of origin, as the vegetables come from the farm to our table as they are, without any packaging. They are 'food with the farmer's face on it', as the name of the first Japanese CSAs translates. The mutual trust between the farmer and the members is the guarantee. What I have experienced and observed is highly redolent with what leisure studies has embraced: the notion of leisure as resistance (e.g. Shaw 2001; Mair [2002] 2003), food as a key concept with an overtly political character (Harris 2005) and eating 'as a locus for reflection, resistance, and the articulation of alternatives – the essence of political practice' (Mair, Sumner, and Rotteau 2008, 385).

Our CSA challenges and rearticulates dominant ideological understandings not only about food but health as well. There are a lot of conversations going on within the community where people express their opposition towards the state health care system, medicalization or what Beck calls a 'risk society' (Beck, Giddens, and Lash 1994, 6), and share ideas about alternative medical practices, or recommend alternative health care to each other. Sometimes I can do nothing but agree with them. However, I feel myself in a 'schizophrenic' position. Health promotion can be seen as representing the state and bureucray and to some extent the commodification of health, while my CSA membership can be interpreted within a social, environmental movement towards the decommodification of health and food which constitutes a political act. What I can do is to build my experiences into my university work but I agree with Labonte (1994) that vehicles must exist or be created through which social movement knowledge can be translated into broader sectors. Understanding the causes of these social movements 'may help [scholars and citizens as well] to engage the politics of popular culture and to craft, refine, and put into action alternatives that benefit everyone' (Mair, Sumner, and Rotteau 2008, 400).

I am more than satisfied with the vegetables we get from the farm but as with other members, the question also arises in me: where to get healthy local fruit, dairy products or meat. It is again a step for the community towards taking more control over our food/ system and health. Both health promotion (e.g., Kickbusch 2010) and leisure scholars (e. g., Mair, Sumner, and Rotteau 2008) would say that our community is more and more empowered. Finally, the farmers make agreement with two local producers to sell organic fruit to the community members during the time of the pick-ups.

Our CSA is not only characterized by its resistance to the consumer market ideology, but it has a proactive, visionary sense of new social and economic relationships. If we accept that unchecked capitalism has contributed to the degradation of our agriculture and gastronomy, 'the remedy is not to be found in the marketplace, but rather in a set of spaces and practices that abandon the reductionist logic of the market altogether' (Dunlap 2012, 42). I have found practices that are not characteristic of the capitalist market. The farmers' dominant rhetoric involves gift and gifting. In the farmer-customer agreement and other farm documents there are references to gifting: the farmer's as being gifted by having a community around them; offering their knowledge as a gift to the community; nature giving us its gifts every week. This rhetoric is so powerful that it infuses our communication within the community. Once we were asked by the farmer how we could be even more contented, and a bunch of people including me assured him that we accept every kind of vegetable we get from the farm, may they be curved, grubby or a bit woody (but they rarely are so). We do not measure them. But why is it that my otherwise overly critical disposition is kept at bay? Because we do not take these vegetables as commodities but rather as gifts, the gifts of nature. Following Hyde's (2007) interpretation of gift – which is a freely made gesture to maintain the flow of resources – to measure, reckon value or to make a cost–benefit analysis would mean to step outside the cycle of the gift. If I did not feel like this, I would find Hyde's (2007) words too sentimental, 'the gift [...] when it comes speaks commandingly to the soul and irresistibly moves us' (xvii). It is this creative spirit of the gift that establishes bonds among us and we feel obliged to accept, give and reciprocate this gift; commodities do not have this nature and they rather disconnect people according to Hyde (2007). It is this continuous act of giving and receiving gifts within which sustainability questions can be explained and interpreted: we do recycling and composting because we feel obliged to do so, to make the gift flow.

All these features show that our community has elements of what is called a gift community. This version of CSA evolved from Steinerian roots and according to Ravenscroft et al. (2012), it 'involves farmers, community and land working intensely together' (9) as they all constitute an organism and 'is characterised by a strong ethic of care and [...] by community connections that insist on linking health, food and community security' (9). The farmers say that 'this is not our work to earn money, this is our life' which is consistent with this version of CSA according to Jarosz (2011). They do not want to make a huge profit; they just want to live with the land and not from the land. It is also within this notion of gift community that 'the shared risks and rewards' can be interpreted. Because of a storm, we were left without gooseberries but the farm compensated us with the bounty of summer squash. To enter into a human–nature gift relationship means that the effects of this relationship cannot be predicted or even controlled. We experience the ways in which we are connected to Nature; we are not lords of it but parts of it. We are far away from the efficiency, calculability, predictability and control of McDonaldization, Ritzer's (2003) symbolic notion for capitalist consumer culture.

At the end of September, 12 of us are invited for a core group formation meeting by the farmers. As the email says 'a core group is responsible for working out the details of the CSA, it spreads the workload and its operation decreases the likelihood of the farmer's burnout. Activities may include crop selection; payment schedules; organizing distribution, volunteer activities, and special events'. I am honoured to be invited and when I arrive at the meeting I find 10 keen members and the farmers who think it is time to delegate some tasks to members. To the best of our knowledge, there is no core group at any other Hungarian CSA. It is both a challenge and responsibility for us. Right at the beginning we find a playful, untranslatable name to give the group an identity. Ideas are pouring, we prove to be a highly inspirational and creative bunch of people. As a result of the group's activity, the recipe blog is being added by the vegetable biographies to educate members and the organization of the volunteer work at the distribution is also referred to the care of the core group. The weekly meetings usually last well into the evening, so after a month or so I am having a disagreement with my husband about unmet familial commitments, a clear indication that I devote quite a lot of time to my core group activity, a devotional practice as Blackshaw (2010) would call it.

I remember that several months ago, I was asked to fill out a questionnaire about Hungarian CSAs. When asked about the positive outcomes of being a member, I gave a 5 on a 1–5 Likert scale in the category of 'chance for leisure activities'; however, I was puzzled by the wording. For me the whole thing seems to mean leisure, not just one or two activities associated with it so I added the following:

> It is hard to define and categorize the positive outcomes of being a member, but I would say what captured me was the spirituality of this whole thing and that a CSA initiative is a good thing and being involved in it is extremely good. I firmly believe that CSAs can give a useful and meaningful devotion to people besides the fresh and high quality vegetable.

Autumn, with a lot of work in our CSA, gives me an opportunity to lament on my thoughts. On an October pick-up day, it is my turn to help with the distribution. I do this with joy and pleasure. I enjoy socializing with members, help them, I do it for good reasons, for the community, for the ideal of the CSA, something which is beyond my own interest. Every movement I do – taking out empty boxes to the car, cleaning the tables, sweeping the hallway of the school – is a meaningful, truly human activity for me. The small gesture of sweeping gives me a true experience. A real lived experience. As Blackshaw (2010) puts it:

> We need to get greedy for the small, true details of life that leisure offers us. It is only when we are able to grasp the possibility that we will be able to step clear of consumer cluttered lives into a new relationship with ourselves and the world, one which is at once simpler and more profound than the liquid life pursued under what current conditions allow. (149)

I may seem to be too sentimental, but I would say that my movement has something sacred in it, 'as if it were something holy, as though engaging in it were a religious function' (Blackshaw 2010, 141). This is not the same sweeping I do in my courtyard, or to be more precise, it is the same act but with a different meaning. And the meaning seems to be more important than the action itself. This is consistent with the findings of Ravenscroft: the meanings behind the activities of CSA members were much greater than the significance of the activities themselves (Ravenscroft et al. 2013). This means that Blackshaw (2010, 141) is right when he says 'leisure has become a hermeneutical exercise'.

For me and the core group, the whole of October is about preparing for the approaching Saint Martin feast, to invite the staff of the Waldorf School to say thank you for hosting the community's pick up. We are throwing ourselves into the preparation wholeheartedly, it is the first project coordinated by the core group. I decide to contribute to the feast with a presentation on the spiritual aspects of CSAs. I am burying myself into the legend of Saint Martin whose feast marks the end of the agricultural year. I am concentrating on what his simple and modest life can teach us – something that the Beijing Consensus also addresses. I am preparing to speak about the flow of the gift to make the Steinerian rooted gift community work.

In spite of our enthusiasm, other preparations do not seem to go very well as the members are not so willing to offer food for the potluck. For weeks, it seems that the core group would host the staff, quite a disappointment for one or two core group members. I am not impatient, community does not build spontaneously. We speak about how this membership has formed a new identity for us. And that 'other' people cannot understand our delight in CSA. What others see as inconveniences and constraints in the system, I regard as self imposed limitations, markers of my freedom. Or to quote Blackshaw (2010, 150) 'since freedom imposes no constraints on us to find it, we need to impose some kind of constraints on ourselves'. In the end, we change our way of communication towards the community and we present the event to the members as an offering and not as a duty. This seems to have worked because when I arrive at the school, I find long rows of tables loaded with cakes, pumpkins, salads and other delicious things and candles burn among them against the growing darkness of the season, a tradition at Saint Martin's Feast. I do not bring any food; however, I feel that with my presentation I can contribute to the intellectual and spiritual development of the farm, to make an ideal realized – 'my artful living' as Blackshaw (2010) would call it.

Winter

December greets us with unusually warm weather, but the boxes full of heavy pumpkins, cabbages and root vegetables remind us that the end of the year is approaching. The core group is busy organizing a Christmas celebration for the last pick-up day. We decide on baking gingerbreads for the community and we gather in the home of one of us. I have loads of work to do, still I devote some time to make my contribution to the gingerbread making. I offer my rich collection of colourful ribbons as a decoration for the gingerbreads thinking that these ribbons symbolize our connectedness. Again it is my turn to be the volunteer helper at the last pick-up. The registration table is loaded with gingerbreads of different shapes and decorations. People seem to be impressed by both the gesture and the beauty of our creations, some of them take a long time selecting from the different gingerbreads. We overestimated the quantity needed, so it happens that our small Christmas tree at home is almost exclusively decorated with the gingerbreads – fully articulating my identity. And the ribbon of the gingerbread reminds me of the wording of the Beijing Consensus: leisure as 'a soft ribbon that gently connects people's material life to their spiritual life' (2010). These Christmas ribbons become the representation of my leisure connecting my material and spritual life.

The new year starts with a dilemma for the farmers and they ask the core group to discuss the matter. Some retailers see an opportunity for selling their products at the time of the pick-ups. We are more and more like a marketplace and the question arises whether this is what the farmers and the community want. The core group unanimously rejects consumerism. Principles are worked out about who is allowed to sell what kind of products and when. This is a crucial point in the development of the community. It is a clear standpoint that time and space should be devoted to the community and not to consumption. We also agree that each member has the right to participate in decision-making. The foundation of a participatory democracy is being laid down here. Our involvement in the communal life of our CSA reminds me of the Greek leisure ideal. For the polis members, leisure was the arena where civility was cultivated and where many spheres of human activity were conjoined: the political, the social, the economic and the cultural (Hemingway 1988). Rojek's (2001) 'life politics' or Mair's 'civil leisure' ([2002] 2003) also draw our attention to the relationship between leisure and citizenship rights. Far from being a passive consumer, CSA members can take up an active political role in their leisure and they can become the co-producer of their own food and thus contribute to social change. It is communities like ours and their communal leisure practice that Arai and Pedlar (2003, 199) redirect our attention to in leisure studies emphasizing the importance of these communities in 'confront[ing] the social and political crises in (post) modern democratic capitalist countries'.

While the farm rests in winter, and there are only stored vegetables to be distributed among members, the soil seems to be lifeless but a closer look would reveal the rich interconnectedness of the soil web; millions of organisms are doing their job just like the core group is busy in the background preparing for the spring season. We are making a questionnaire to evaluate last year and we are brainstorming about the development of the recipe blog. While we are doing this, I challenge the others with the question whether it is work or leisure for them. Some of them are puzzled by it and would choose neither. Some say, it is something like volunteer work, still others hold that it is satisfying work done for their own pleasure and for the community. These constructions are close to 'civil labour' (Rojek 2001), which 'refers to voluntarily chosen socially neccessary labour' (122). With this notion, Rojek (2001) does not neutralize leisure but calls for a revison between work, the individual and society because 'the distinction between leisure and the rest of life is untenable' (123). All core group members are women on maternity leave and/or self-employed with the exception of me. Most of us see our CSA membership as a coherent part of our wider lives and view it as a personal project to become more aware and conscious parents, teachers, etc., and competent, relevant and credible citizens (Rojek 2010). This way leisure for us ceases to be the reward for work, it is rather a site for self-development and for civic participation that enhances care for the self and care for the other (Rojek 2010). As one member tells, 'it is not about what we do, but rather that we do it together'. Unlike paid emloyment in the market society which carries the connotation of burden, these work experiences are satisfying, creative and productive, and they are key contributions to social capital (Rojek 2001). To put together Rojek and Hyde, civil labour puts constraints on individual choice and freedom, such as a gift community puts constraints on members, but 'these assure the freedom of the gift' (Hyde 2007, 126).

The coldness and darkness of winter give me the opportunity to turn inside, to comtemplate what I have been given from my CSA, what I have gained, and to take a look at my membership from a health and leisure perspective. First I have more insight into the food system as a key determinant of health. Being a CSA member means an opportunity to understand interconnectedness among food governance, production and consumption and to arrive at a whole-systems way of thinking. Being part of a local food system, I can contribute to my family's health and that of the environment. I also started to live in the seasons, follow my emotions and have meaningful rituals around the agricultural year. From the leisure perspective, I started to see eating as a pleasurable empowering practice which constitutes a political act. My membership is a way for me to search for meaning and to try to go beyond postmodern individualization and grab the meaning of life which is the meaning of leisure (Blackshaw 2010). My CSA membership creates an artful living. This is what it means to me to be in harmony with myself, with others and with nature. CSA creates a space where I can live an authentic and healthy life, a spiritual thriving towards everything which is beautiful, truthful and good. The sheer idea of CSA warms my heart.

I look out of the window onto our garden and I see some tree buds…

Acknowledgement

This manuscript has greatly benefited from the comments of reviewers for this *Journal*.

Notes

1. Associations pour le maintien d'une Agriculture paysanne, Associations for the protection of small-scale farming.
2. However, Hungarian CSAs bear the hallmarks of an AMAP, there are some modifications so that the system fits more to the Hungarian conditions (see later for example of payment conditions). Throughout the paper, I am going to use the term CSA and vegetable community to refer to my CSA.

References

Adler, P. A., and P. Adler. 1994. "Observational Techniques." In *Handbook of Qualitative Research*, edited by N. K. Denzin and Y. S. Lincoln, 377–392. Thousand Oaks, CA: Sage.

Anderson, M. D., and J. T. Cook. 2000. "Does Food Security Require Local Food Systems?" In *Rethinking Sustainability: Power, Knowledge and Institutions*, edited by J. M. Harris, 228–248. Ann Arbor: University of Michigan Press.

Arai, S., and A. Pedlar. 2003. "Moving beyond Individualism in Leisure Theory: A Critical Analysis of Concepts of Community and Social Engagement." *Leisure Studies* 22 (3): 185–202. doi:10.1080/026143603200075489.

Beck, U., A. Giddens, and S. Lash. 1994. *Reflexive Modernization: Politics, Tradition and Aesthetics in the Modern Social Order*. New York: Stanford University Press.

Behar, R. 1996. *The Vulnerable Observer: Anthropology that Breaks Your Heart*. Boston, MA: Beacon Press.

Benkő, Zs. 2005. "Bevezetés az egészségfejlesztésbe [Introduction to Health Promotion]." In *Iskolai egészségfejlesztés* [School Health Promotion], edited by Zs. Benkő and K. Tarkó, 13–27. Szeged: JGYF Kiadó.

Benkő, Zs., K. Tarkó, and L. Lippai, eds. 2013. *Leisure, Health and Well-being. Conference Abstracts*. Szeged: Juhász Gyula Faculty of Education, Institute of Applied Health Sciences and Health Promotion, University of Szeged.

Benkő, Zs., K. Tarkó, K. Erdei, and L.Lippai. 2009. "Hagyomány és modernitás a 'Visegrádi négyek' családjainak életmódjában; Táplálkozási szokások [Tradition and Modernity in the Lifestyle of the Families of the Visegrad Countries; Eating Habits]." In *Tudományos és művészeti műhelymunkák* [Academic and Artistic Workshops], edited by Sz. Tóth, 410–414. Szeged: SZTE JGYPK, Garamond 2000.

Berry, W. 1990. *What Are People for?* New York: North Point Press.

Blackshaw, T. 2010. *Leisure*. Abingdon: Routledge.

Büscher, B., S. Sullivan, K. Neves, J. Igoe, and D. Brockington. 2012. "Towards a Synthesized Critique of Neoliberal Biodiversity Conservation." *Capitalism Nature Socialism* 23 (2): 4–30. doi:10.1080/10455752.2012.674149.

Cohen, L., S. Larijani, M. Aboelata, and L. Mikkelsen. 2004. *Cultivating Common Ground. Linking Health and Sustainable Agriculture*. Oakland, CA: Prevention Institute.

De Grazia, S. 1964. *Of Time, Work, and Leisure*. New York: Twentieth Century Fund/Anchor Books.

Dunlap, R. 2012. "Recreating Culture: Slow Food as a Leisure Education Movement." *World Leisure Journal* 54 (1): 38–47. doi:10.1080/04419057.2012.668038.

Girou, S. 2008. "Collective farm shops and AMAP (French CSA) in southwest France. Commitment and Delegation on the Part of Producers and Consumers." Paper presented at 2nd Sustainable Consumption an Alternative Agrifood Systems Conference, Arlon, May 27–30.

Glesne, C., and A. Peshkin. 1992. *Becoming Qualitative Researchers: An Introduction*. White Plains, NY: Longman.

Groh, T., and S. McFadden. 1997. *Farms of Tomorrow Revisited*. Kimberton, PA: Biodynamic Farming and Gardening Association.

Harris, D. 2005. *Key Concepts in Leisure Studies*. London: Sage.

Harvey, D. 2005. *A Brief History of Neoliberalism*. Oxford: Oxford University Press.

Hemingway, J. L. 1988. "Lesiure and Civility: Reflections on a Greek Ideal." *Leisure Sciences* 10 (3): 179–191. doi:10.1080/01490408809512188.

Henderson, E. 2010. "The World of Community Supported Agriculture." Paper presented at the 4th URGENCI International Symposium on Community Supported Foods and Farming, Kobe, February 22.

Henderson, E., and R. Van En. 2007. *Sharing the Harvest: A Citizen's Guide to Community Supported Agriculture*. White River Junction, VT: Chelsea Green Publishing Company.

Hinrichs, C. 2000. "Embeddedness and Local Food Systems: Notes on Two Types of Direct Agricultural Market." *Journal of Rural Studies* 16 (3): 295–303. doi:10.1016/S0743-0167(99)00063-7.

Honoré, C. 2004. *In Praise of Slowness: How a Worldwide Movement is Challenging the Cult of Speed*. New York: HarperSanFrancisco.

Hyde, L. 2007. *The Gift. Creativity and the Artist in the Modern World*. New York: Vintage.

International Sociological Association Research Committee on Sociology of Leisure. 2010. "Beijing Consensus on Leisure Civilization." In *Leisure and Civilization: Interdisciplinary and International Perspectives*, edited by I. Modi, M. Huidi, and N. Zequn, 232–234. Beijing: China Travel and Tourism Press.

Jarosz, L. 2011. "Nourishing Women: Toward a Feminist Political Ecology of Community Supported Agriculture in the United States." *Gender, Place and Culture* 18 (3): 307–326. doi:10.1080/0966369X.2011.565871.

Kelly, J. R. 1996. *Leisure*. 3rd ed. Boston, MA: Allyn & Bacon.

Kickbusch, I. 2010. *The Food System: A Prism for Present and Future Challenges for Health Promotion and Sustainable Development Triggering Debate: White Paper*. Geneva: Health Promotion Switzerland.

Labonte, R. 1994. *Health Promotion and Empowerment. Practice Frameworks*. Toronto: Centre for Health Promotion, University of Toronto.

Lippai, L. 2007. "Free Time." In *Tradition and Modernity in the Life-Style of the Families of the Visegrád Countries*, edited by Zs. Benkő, 79–90. Szeged: Juhász Gyula Felsőoktatási Kiadó.

Mair, H. [2002] 2003. "Civil Leisure? Exploring the Relationship between Leisure, Activism and Social Change." *Leisure/Loisir* 27 (3/4): 213–237. doi:10.1080/14927713.2002.9651304.

Mair, H., J. Sumner, and L. Rotteau. 2008. "The Politics of Eating: Food Practices as Critically Reflexive Leisure." *Leisure/Loisir* 32 (2): 379–405. doi:10.1080/14927713.2008.9651415.

Ravenscroft, N., N. Moore, E. Welch, and A. Church. 2012. *Connecting Communities through Food: The Theoretical Foundations of Community Supported Agriculture in the UK*. CRESC Working Paper Series Working Paper No. 115. Manchester: The University of Manchester.

Ravenscroft, N., M. Moore, E. Welch, and R. Hanney. 2013. "Beyond Agriculture: The Counter-Hegemony of Community Farming." *Agriculture and Human Values*, 30 (4): 629–639. doi:10.1007/s10460-013-9437-7.

Réthy, K., and Z. Dezsény. 2013. *Közösség által támogatott mezőgazdaság. Útmutató gazdálkodóknak a rövid élelmiszerláncokról és a termelői-fogyasztói közösségek létrehozásáról* [Community-supported Agriculture. Instructions for Farmers on Establishing Short Supply Chains and Farmer-producer Communities]. Ökológiai Mezőgazdasági Kutatóintézet Közhasznú Nonprofit Kft (ÖMKI).

Ritzer, G. 2003. *Contemporary Social Theory and Its Classical Roots: The Basics.* New York: McGraw Hill.

Roberts, K. 2011. "Leisure: The Importance of Being Inconsequential." *Leisure Studies* 30 (1): 5–20. doi:10.1080/02614367.2010.506650.

Rojek, C. 1995. *Decentring Leisure: Rethinking Leisure Theory.* London: Sage.

Rojek, C. 2001. "Leisure and Life Politics." *Leisure Sciences: An Interdisciplinary Journal* 23 (2): 115–125. doi:10.1080/014904001300181701.

Rojek, C. 2010. *The Labour of Leisure.* London: Sage.

Saltmarsh, N., J. Meldrum, and N. Longhurst. 2011. *The Impact of Community Supported Agriculture: Final Report.* Bristol: Soil Association.

Shaw, S. 2001. "Conceptualizing Resistance: Women's Leisure as Political Practice." *Journal of Leisure Research* 33 (2): 186–201.

Slater, D. 1998. "Work/Leisure." In *Core Sociological Dichotomies*, edited by C. Jenks, 391–405. London: Sage.

Tranter, P. J. 2010. "Speed Kills: The Complex Links between Transport, Lack of Time and Urban Health." *Journal of Urban Health* 87 (2): 155–166. doi:10.1007/s11524-009-9433-9.

Vadovics, E., and M. Hayes. 2007. "Nyitott Kert – egy helyi bioélelmiszer-hálózat Magyarországon [Open Garden – A Local Organic Producer-consumer Network in Hungary]." In *Fenntartható fogyasztás Magyarországon* [Sustainable Development in Hungary], edited by E. Vadovics and E. Gulyás, 237–258. Tudományos konferencia. Konferenciakötet.

World Health Organisation. 1986. "Ottawa Charter for Health Promotion." *Health Promotion International* 1: ii–v. doi:10.4278/0890-1171-1-1-ii.

World Health Organisation. 2005. *The Bangkok Charter for Health Promotion in a Globalized World.* Geneva.

Magical activism: what happens between the worlds changes the worlds

Cris Calley Jones and Heather Mair

Department of Recreation and Leisure Studies, University of Waterloo, Waterloo, ON, Canada

Witch camps are part of a contemporary philosophical and spiritual movement that encourages social, political and environmental activism. Through an examination of the witch camp experience, this paper highlights the lived intersections of alternative spirituality, community and activism in leisure. Using a critical constructionist, qualitative design, data were collected through participant observation at 2 witch camps, 21 semi-structured intensive interviews, 11 focused interviews and 19 elicited electronic text submissions. Findings illustrate how camp functions as a container for personal and social transformation and provides an 'antidote' to alienation and isolation experienced by individuals in the mainstream. The notion of magical activism captures both the experience of the participants and the connection between personal and social transformation in this context. The paper provides empirical evidence of the centrality of leisure and spirituality in engendering responsibility for broader social, political and environmental issues.

Introduction

Each year, Witch camps rise up like little Brigadoons across the face of Gaia. Communities form as stars from the scattered dust of our diaspora, each of us drawn by the irresistible power of love, and our belief that Magic is real and can transform the world. More than Pagan festivals, Witch camps are intensive spiritual retreats that are nevertheless great fun. Each camp is created in sacred space and provides a safe venue for practicing Magic and exploring the myriad ways to connect to the divine within us all. Each is a place where mundane inhibitions fall away and our true Selves can emerge and be celebrated ... Skyclad bodies leaping in the firelight, whirling figures in flowing robes fanning the flames, drummers beating a frenzied rhythm, Witches dancing their passion for life in this amazingly beautiful world, each heart a blaze of prayer. Young and old, women and men – gay, lesbian, straight, bi and trans – the music moves each to dance in their own way. Each brings to the circle their art, their music, their culture, and their own unique voice. (Wolf 2006, 7)

As part of a contemporary philosophical and spiritual movement that encourages social, political and environmental justice, and as an understudied phenomenon, witch camps provide an opportunity to explore the lived intersections of spirituality, community, activism and leisure. Witch camps, Wicca, Witchcraft and modern Paganism have received limited attention, albeit from a variety of disciplines including ethnographic theology (Salomonsen 2002), anthropology (Greenwood 2000; Hume 1997; Rountree 2004), folklore (Magliocco 2004) and sociology (Berger 2005), and in a variety of

Western cultures including New Zealand, Australia, Great Britain and America. However, they have not been examined as a unique entity and experience, nor much considered within a leisure framework (Calley Jones 2010).

We were interested in leisure as a vehicle for social and political change and had encountered the assertion that spirituality is a critical factor in how people relate to the earth, as well as being a motivating force for activism (Ammerman 1997; Cerny 2004; Holloway 2003; Kong 2001; Shaw 2004; Van Schyndel Kasper 2008). Our purpose with this critical constructionist research was to capture and describe the richness, complexities and tensions within witch camp participants' experiences and to theorize about the primary elements. Data analysis revealed three primary elements, which focused on how participants situated the camp experience in their lives, the meanings they constructed from the experience and whether (and how) they linked their experience to broader social change. We argue the alternative culture of witch camps not only provides an 'antidote' to alienation and isolation experienced by individuals in contemporary society, but also it functions as a container for the development of personal and social transformation. Further, we provide empirical evidence that the witch camp experience reinforces the centrality of leisure in engendering responsibility for addressing broader social, political and environmental issues.

As critical constructionist researchers, we entered the project with guiding interests (Charmaz 2006) rather than firm concepts to identify or pursue. The following section reviews briefly these guiding interests.

Literature review

Witchcraft and witch camps

Given the popular mystification and misconceptions in regard to Witchcraft and these kinds of gatherings, we offer a brief introduction to the event and the culture (see also Calley Jones 2010). The following excerpt is adapted from the website of the Witch Camps Council:

> Witch camps are intensive retreats for the study of Magic and ritual, and are offered to women, men, and families, at all levels of experience. Within a mythological and historical framework of the Goddess Tradition, newcomers can learn the basic skills of Magic and ritual, and learn to bend the elements of earth, air, fire, and water. Advanced paths (workshops) offer teachings to apply ritual tools (trance work, drumming, dancing, chanting, storytelling, guided visualization, energy work) to personal healing and empowerment, or to apply the craft to healing issues surrounding power and leadership in the world through public ritual and smaller learning groups. Reclaiming Witchcraft values diversity and each Witch camp has its own policies, structures, and culture. Transparency is encouraged and valued, as is a questioning attitude. (witchcamp.org)

Witch camps can be located within what Hume (1997) describes as Paganism/Wicca/ Witchcraft, a philosophical and decentralized movement that synthesizes ecology, spirituality and science. Within Western cultures, Witchcraft is growing and flourishing (Berger 2005) and appears to be multiplying exponentially among teens and young adults (De Souza 2003; Cush 2007). Witch camps originated in San Francisco in 1985 (Magliocco 2004) as a contrivance of the Reclaiming Tradition of Witchcraft, a tradition referred to as an 'accidental institution' (Starhawk 2011, 262) with a commitment to the natural world, social justice and political activism (Berger 2005). Reclaiming is a decentralized group with origins in the highly creative 1970s explorations of feminist spirituality, consciousness shifting and new age mentality (Starhawk 2011). The first witch camp outside of California took place in British Columbia in 1987. According to Starhawk (2011), the goal with the first camps was to seed magical communities locally and to teach and empower local leadership.

There are 15–20 witch camps scattered throughout the USA, Canada, Western Europe, and most recently, Australia and each camp focuses less or more on spirit, environment or politics. They are annual events and depending on the preferences of the local organizing group, each one incorporates a theme, story or myth as a vehicle for creative consciousness-raising about particular social, environmental or political problems and celebrations of life. Most are held in a rustic camp setting, operate collectively and work to be environmentally friendly. During camps, individuals primarily live communally and are intensely immersed in pathwork (facilitated group work focused on community building, eco/magical skills and connecting with the local landscape) and rituals that explore the Reclaiming Tradition beliefs and practices (Berger 2005).

Witch camps might be considered an emergent form of leisure (Rojek, Shaw, and Veal 2006) demonstrated by their novelty and in their existence as sites and practice of opposition to hegemonic codes of behaviour, as well as their attempts to envision environmental and cultural change. As is discussed below, Cris has a history in the shared leadership of a witch camp, and so was aware of the efforts and tensions that arise around planning camps that are environmentally friendly, feminist, affordable, welcoming to all cultures, traditions, genders and sexualities, include developmentally appropriate events for children and teens and offer a full range of diet options.

While costuming is not expected, it is widespread. In the spirit of reclaiming the image of the Witch, some campers appear in the garb of the common Witch stereotype, complete with pointy hat, black cloak and broom. Generally, however, the attire is a fantastic collection of various hats and cloaks that involve a range of high-tech outdoor gear, wildly colourful fabrics and playful body décor.

Festivals

Festivals are a social phenomenon universal to all human cultures and function primarily to renounce or announce culture, to renew sense of community and to affirm its institutions (Falassi 1967). Likely originating as ancient seasonal occasions of public joy and merriment, festivals provide a break from mundane life and an opportunity to honour the mystical and spiritual in shared community. In the way that dreams and fantasy are indispensable to mental health, the fantastic culture of festivals is necessary for the social health of a community (Turner 1982) and is an active force in social change (Waterman 1998). Festivals play a key role in creating, maintaining, transforming and transmitting culture (Waterman 1998). Western festivals have evolved and fragmented into a multiplicity of forms such as fairs, family feasts, arts, music, cultural festivals, religious events, parties and even what we refer to as the 'weekend' (Abrahams 1982). A primary characteristic of festivals is the creation of spatial, temporal and social openness, where participants are invited to explore the margins of typical social interaction and try on personal and social transformations that may or may not be carried back to the real world (Falassi 1967). Although not all festivals have a stated social change purpose, they are set apart from 'regular' life and are positioned in the broader social context such that they do not need to actively promote social change in order to affect it (Sharpe 2008).

The largest witch camps draw about 125 people, paltry compared to the thousands that attend some cultural or music festivals. Nonetheless, witch camps can be located within this festival framework in that they provide an occasion for the community to gather outside of normal life to publicly display, explore, affirm and transform itself (Abrahams 1982; Falassi 1967). A number of studies have looked at festivals that share characteristics of being for and by marginalized communities based on gender (Eder, Staggenborg, and Sudderth 1995; Morris 2005), race and culture (Jackson 1992), sexual orientation (Browne 2007) or political viewpoint (Sharpe 2008). Each festival is understood as creating space and time for alternative social interaction and transformation, and this scholarship indicates festivals are spaces of resistance to, and/or reproduction of, cultural norms and events that blend pleasure with politics.

Pike (2001) situated Pagan festivals within what she called the American historical tradition of blending religion and leisure and noted that Pagan festivals tend to contest accepted cultural norms by supporting alternative values. As a result, they are powerful places of meaning-making for those whose interests lie outside the dominant norms. Berger (2005) describes Pagan festivals as summer camps for adults as attendants gain a sense of spiritual community with those who share their worldview, and they participate in a temporary prefigurative community. For Berger, witch camps can be differentiated from other Pagan festivals by their specific expression of the Reclaiming Tradition of Witchcraft's feminist, non-hierarchical leadership and their focus on the political, personal and spiritual. She also distinguishes witch camps by their nurturance of natural rather than chemically induced altered states of consciousness and by their rejection of polarity based on gender (a heteronormative belief that male = masculine/God and female = feminine/Goddess) as both are necessary for ritual Magic. A final distinction is that witch camps prioritize honouring the earth through Magical and environmental activism. Salomonsen (2002) summarized the camps as sites of healing from alienation through spirituality in community, as well as places where Witches learn to 'bend' or transform human consciousness and develop personally (see also Magliocco 2004).

Leisure, social change and spirituality

Shaw (2001) led us to consider resistance, which illuminates the political nature and potential of leisure as a space of social change. Shaw argued that leisure, defined as a situation of choice, control, individual agency and self-determination, provides opportunity for individuals who are marginalized or oppressed to reproduce, or resist, proscribed roles, expectations and behaviours. Related to intentional resistance is civil leisure (Mair 2002), a notion rooted in Hemingway's (1999) conceptualization of leisure as a context for social justice and human emancipation. Involving a sense of duty to the greater public good, civil leisure highlights freely chosen activities such as activism, civil disobedience, public protest and politically oriented festivals; all public activities with a social change message (see also, Gilchrist and Ravenscroft 2013; Lashua 2005; Sharpe 2008). Mair, Sumner, and Rotteau (2008) further refine intentional resistance with critically reflexive leisure, which refers to politically oriented leisure including reflection, resistance and the articulation of an alternative vision informed by pleasure, activism and empowerment.

However, scholarship on leisure and social change has virtually ignored the role of spirituality. As leisure-based, festival-style communities built on an assumption of shared Pagan spirituality, community and a politic that promotes activism, witch camps provide a rare opportunity to explore the claim that spirituality is a motivating force in social justice activism (Cerny 2004; Holloway 2003; Kong 2001; Shaw 2004; Van Schyndel Kasper 2008). Researchers suggests those who include the earth in their understandings of community and spirituality are more likely to act in accordance with those values, treat their environments gently (Van Schyndel Kasper 2008) and are more likely to take a protective stance (Shaw 2004). As Ammerman (1997) argues, religious and spiritual communities are often the social spaces where people learn civic skills and practices that are then carried into other areas of life.

This review pinpoints our need to better understand how spirituality, leisure and social change intersect in so-called alternative cultures where individuals and communities work to resist, renounce and/or reproduce the dominant culture. Of course, we must resist the tendency to romanticize these cultures as they can create a heady cauldron rife with tensions including conflicting and unclear goals and agendas. Pike (2001) and Morris (2005) reported some of the tensions that can arise when the individual intersects with community and utopian visions intersect with present culture. Nonetheless, deeper understandings can be developed through an exploration of the experiences and the tensions, and opportunities abound for appreciating their potential when viewed as more than mere cultural aberrations.

Methodological approach and analysis

Study participants were recruited in a number of ways. An initial invitation to participate was posted to electronic mailing lists associated with the camps. Next, Cris attended two witch camps in 2010, one each in Ontario, Canada and Missouri, USA, in order to undertake participant observation and to recruit participants. She had assured camp organizers she would be careful not to disrupt the camp experience and so at both camps, she requested time at the orientation meeting to introduce herself and the study and to invite interested participants to contact her if they were willing to be involved. She let the campers know she would be observing and taking notes but that she would also be a full camp participant. Additional participants were recruited through invitation, snowball and purposive sampling.

Data collection, undertaken by Cris, first included semi-structured, intensive, individual interviews with 21 present and past witch camp participants, which were audio-taped (with consent), and used open-ended questions about the meanings of camp. Fourteen of the intensive interviews were conducted in the camp setting and seven were conducted away from the camps. These interviews lasted between two and three hours. This process then evolved to include an additional 11 focused, shorter interviews (under an hour) conducted outside the camp setting and undertaken after preliminary data analysis of the intensive interviews in order to elicit narratives exploring the individual, the community and their relationship with witch camp. An additional 19 people returned written text, responding electronically to the same questions used in the intensive interviews. All participants have been given pseudonyms, which are used below. The sample included a range of both newer (i.e., at least three camp experiences) and seasoned campers (i.e., up to 20 camps) and was predominantly female, with just two males participating in the interviews and one who self-identified as gender neutral. Children, although present at camps, were excluded from the study.

Insider research describes research involving both a professional and a personal research interest. It is generally carried out in one's own 'backyard' (Glesne and Peshkin 1992) and relies on the advantage of access to the 'backstage culture' (deMunck and Sobo 1998, 43). Cris's social location as an organizer of previous witch camps and experience with the culture of Reclaiming Witchcraft engendered trust relationships, access and helped her gather rich details. Nonetheless, her insider status was a form of power that she employed in accessing the setting and participants. However, her background as a feminist social worker and psychotherapist provided a foundation of training, skills and professional experience, which afforded a critical awareness of the social and political power relationships in the everyday social world. Additionally, as we were aware of the influence of these connections and experiences, participants outside of her immediate circle of friendship were recruited to lessen potential or perceived influence. We also worked together by meeting for regular discussions in order to ensure data analysis maintained a critical perspective and to remain conscious of our privileged status, a process of self-examination that is referred to as critical consciousness (Freire 1970). Like Cris, Heather has a background in feminist and critical approaches to social research and an abiding interest in social movements.

The study on which this paper is based blended Creswell's (2003, 190) systematic steps of data analysis and interpretation with Charmaz's (2006) approach, using both methodological tools as well as the tools of self (insight, reflexivity and ingenuity). From the recording and transcription of interview data, journal notes and observations, through line/segment coding, focused, and theoretical coding, to memo writing, we developed an iterative process, interweaving data analysis and collection (Charmaz, 2006). As gaps in the data were identified during analysis, and/or concepts and categories seemed lacking in rich detail, questions were adjusted for data collection in the next stages.

Findings

Data analysis led to the development of three primary elements underlying the experience of witch camps. First, participants described how camp provided a container, a safe and supportive community, where they could experiment and experience ways of being and living that were alternative – even an antidote – to mainstream life and culture. Next, their experience was clearly connected to personal transformation, if in different and complex ways. Last, participants described deep linkages between what they experienced at camp and how they lived their lives; describing ways of engaging with issues of social change including environmental and social justice. Each of these elements is discussed in turn and then all are interwoven in a discussion of magical activism, a notion capturing the interplay of all three elements and highlighting the unique role of spirituality in social change, alternative culture(s) and leisure.

Creating the container: witch camp community as a crucible for change

Described by participants as 'a container' and 'a resource for change', witch camp functioned as a platform for transformation. For instance, Cruz characterized camp as a:

> container for personal transformation. It's a time and place for looking at myself and identifying things and trying out new ways of being. It ritualizes the shifting into new ways of being, a chance to be my higher self for a continuous stretch of time.

Shechi described a place to move:

> further along my own trajectory of becoming the person I want to be. It's a place of authenticity and stretching. I nurture parts of myself that I value. I see parts of myself emerge. Coming here is a place to step back and set that as an intention. What would it look like in my normal life to remember my power? This is a community I trust to mirror me honestly. Witch camp is a place where I like who I am when I'm here. I think it's somewhat of my better self, my gentler self, my more relaxed self. I have permission to think about a different response to my life.

Beastie said:

> Witch camp can be so irreverent. It brings up play; you can laugh at yourself, and the rest of the world. You are meanwhile doing deep and profound work that enriches your life.

For Wind, camp inspired trust:

> When you are surrounded by people with that kind of energy, it heightens your own openness and awareness. There is an expectation to go deeper than you otherwise would. An expectation to be honest with yourself and see yourself reflected in amazing people that you respect.

Jizak could see aspects of camp experience reflected in her own journey of self-discovery. She said she had felt:

> uncomfortable, like I do not belong at times because there are extroverts who get a lot of attention at witch camp and I sometimes feel left out. I believe this sense of not belonging is my personal work being brought out at camp and it is an important part of facing my shadows. I think that the positive and negative experiences of belonging are great learning I have done about what community is and how groups work. Camp pushes personal buttons and community does not really exist without conflict, especially when it is less hierarchical and striving to be inclusive. I like that everyone helps out and that people are encouraged to be personally responsible for their experience with help available if someone reaches for it.

Banshee shared her opinion that witch camp was not for everyone, as some people were not personally ready for the depth and intensity of transformation:

> I've seen many enter into personal work that's too deep for them, too challenging, that throws them too off balance. People who enter into the work who aren't ready for it can really put a strain on the facilitators and the community.

For Rocky, it was the lack of judgement that made a difference:

> People like to put you in a box and I get so tired of just one acceptable way to be. All of our institutions are based on heteronormativity and patriarchy. It's so pervasive. There is a freedom from those assumptions here; there is inclusivity and diversity, all those things. People come from their hearts and I don't mean emotions, I mean their hearts. They speak their truth. Authentic. There is a generosity and a willingness to share. People are comfortable with their power and their vulnerability. Not that they are exclusive, but sometimes in our world out there, there is a message that vulnerability is not okay.

Most participants expressed a deep appreciation for being in a space and community where they could fully express any aspect of themselves without concern for mainstream social consequences. Beastie said that: 'things are more real, more authentic', at witch camp because of being protected from the outside world. Maebon said:

> at this age, I really want to just be me in the world. I am with my people at camp, there's nothing like it in my mundane world. I just say what I want to say, be open, freer in myself expression.

Shechi appreciated that she could be fully authentic in that she does not even think about being lesbian or hiding that from anyone. Gwin said she, 'felt safe to open up and be myself in a way that I rarely do in the Muggle world'.

It would appear that the container of witch camp provided participants with rare freedom from the assumptions and judgements of mainstream culture, and an opportunity to openly connect with and present a self they may have kept guarded and closeted in ordinary life. Such liberation enabled comfort with vulnerability and self-expression. The culture and structure of camp were described as similar to intense group therapy as it facilitated awareness, reflection and exploration of the deep inner authentic self. The exploration came with the challenges inherent in integration of the shadow-self and not everyone was prepared or ready for such a process. The high level of emotional fluency in the community, along with an abundance of therapists and healers, provided support through the transformation.

Participants also described witch camp as providing an antidote to mainstream culture. Matty described camp as:

> a relief from the dominant culture. It is an antidote to Witches being low on the totem pole in the dominant culture. There are things one can't easily do at home; plus the mundane world gets in the way.

Patsy said that she found camp to be a 'refreshing change from daily life. It's so important to me to be in a place where the regular Western lifestyle and mindset does not predominate'. Similarly, Crystal described camp as, 'a world of its own, with new norms. My personal life and my camp life are complete opposites'. For Rocky, witch camp was, 'a place where people come together and let go of the things that aren't right in the culture'.

Meg articulated specific differences between camp and mainstream culture:

> It's a chance to live in a more consensual, cooperative community. Mainstream society is not organized this way. There is a big disconnect. Camp is a place to recharge and affirm one's life choices that generally run counter to the mainstream beliefs.

Violet saw camp as the sane way of living:

> Witch camp is a unique experience, a community that is trying to live in an ethical way, a spiritual way, and trying to manifest that in reality. Trying on sanity for a week.

Nanny illustrated some of the ways that witch camp acted as an antidote to the dominant culture:

> We are an antidote to mainstream; which is all head and distrusts the body and distrusts emotion. We learn to pay attention to ourselves in a whole new way. Witch camp invites me to settle deeply into awareness of my own body sensations and from there, into a sense of connection with nature; the part of nature that is non-human; into connection with other people not just through words, more energetically. At camp, I have a heightened sensitivity to energy of all kinds and part of that sensitivity comes from being willing to dance freely, swim nude, and dress expressively, and relax into trance, so my awareness gets opened up. That is very different from the caution and conformity that life outside camp seems to demand. Instead of starting from a mentality that restricts me from trusting my intentions and actions, witch camp is more welcoming of me the looser, more open I am. The assumption is that we are naturally a force for good, if we can get out of our own way. We can truly be guided by ourselves as we are when we fully connect with our whole being within the wonder of the universe.

Witch camp is essential for building hope for Beastie:

> Being in this type of society can be really isolating. It's like having a tribe. It gives me hope. I look around and see peeps throwing garbage and they don't care. I work in wildlife

rehabilitation and you'd think people would care more, but they don't. I see how humans affect the world; every animal crisis that comes in there is caused by humans. Going to witch camp helps me believe that there is a possibility of the world changing. And I can connect with people who can help change things.

Affirming identity through personal transformation: witch camp as therapy and growth

Personal transformation was a clear intention in the witch camp community. Growth, supported within the container of community and nature, was valued by many participants. Goals centred on personal and spiritual growth, leadership development, learning ritual arts and exploring Pagan culture. In reference to personal transformation, the term 'therapy camp' was used by participants and generally, but not always, was said with affection.

Tina said that she had never been to formal therapy before going to camp, but grew to rely on camp as a critical opportunity for therapeutic growth and sharing of intense emotion. Maya said witch camp was:

like group therapy, only the Magic adds a lot of fuel. When I realized camp meant being vulnerable around a lot of people, I went out under some trees and sobbed. And then it turned out to be one of the most transformational experiences ever. Camp has lifted me, and shown me a part of myself I would never have known in another way. Yes, I've grown and benefited.

Pye experienced, 'inner personal transformation; it happens through connecting with my deeper inner self and connecting with others and being open to that connection'. Jizak described a:

sense of freedom from the constraints of everyday life that allows me to open up and really look at myself, and my life. I explore who I am and who I want to be. It is therapeutic because I look at myself and set goals and intentions for what I want in my life and what I want to let go of. I benefit by learning new skills for ritual and for living. I've learned communication skills such as determining what is my issue and what is someone else's issue. I feel revitalized at the end of camp and more able to face the world. It helps me to look at myself more honestly and see what I can and should change and what I should appreciate more about myself.

Personal growth can be serious and emotionally painful, but it can also be fun. For Cayo:

it was a week between the worlds to go inside myself and see more about who I am and where I came from. It was therapy, only fun. It was the safest most beautiful, sensual, fun beyond fun place I have ever been. I grew as a person; I gained strength to step into my power. I was nurtured and loved. I found my true sexuality, I made good friends. I loved my body. It changed my life, without being too dramatic.

For Jax, camp was a place of:

personal transformation and valuable insights. Two years ago, Wild Ginger was like a rebirth for me and it really did feel like a rebirth. I felt like I was coming home and a part of me was being born.

Jax had learned to check in with himself daily on both an emotional and psychological level. He credited camps with teaching him balance, self-acceptance, personal insight and profound personal transformation, 'I am a better person because of witch camps. I'm healthier and more stable and balanced'.

Crystal shared how being at camp gave her a feeling of wholeness and well-being that was:

> difficult to explain. Camp and ritual helped set me on the road to overcoming anxiety. I feel so blessed to have been given this opportunity. I carry this experience with me wherever I go and it reminds me that the world I want is possible.

In the language of Jungian psychology, Rocky and Jax talked of how the personal growth experience of camp had included finding and taking responsibility for one's unconscious or repressed 'shadow-self'. For Rocky, there were, 'costs, such as when I look at my shadow and see things that I'm not comfortable with. But that's really a good thing' Jax said that he was 'not always delighted', by what he learned about himself:

> We can consult with our spiritual selves and not like what we hear. I've seen aspects of myself that were dark and shadowy, and I've felt strongly connected with archetypes that are unappealing and frightening. It's all about who you are and what you bring to the experience.

Tree, who preferred other aspects of camp beyond the therapy aspect, said:

> the whole idea of therapy camp used to just piss me off. Why do you need to do all that personal growth work in order to do Magic? I continue to struggle with that concept though now I'm softer about it. I have an eco-spiritual relationship with the Earth. Camp is about my eco-ethic and the Magic is the spiritual extension of my eco-ethic. Eco-ethics are the base of my spirituality and that relationship is more important to me than therapy camp.

Bruxa playfully summed up our discussion of personal growth at witch camp:

> Sometimes, it's a growth experience, sometimes not. You don't necessarily go and have an epiphany every time. Sometimes you have the big E, sometimes you don't!

Linked to the first theme, and given participants' sense of being closeted in the dominant culture, personal authenticity was highly valued. Camp was a space of authenticity where a Witch could be completely 'out of the broom closet' not only in practice but also in her deepest self. This culture of personal and spiritual authenticity invited, inspired and catalyzed transformation aimed at expression of a genuine self. According to Sequoia, 'to be a Witch means to deal honestly and authentically with every situation in my life. Wherever I am.' Tina, at 56, was 'pretty comfortable', with who she was, but still valued camp as a place where she was her:

> best possible self. That's why I go. I feel authentic. Every messy part that I am, and every great part that I am, is okay. There is lots of permission there.

Violet described herself as:

> a rather eccentric and weird person, who did not fit well with mainstream: social niceties. Witch camp feeds my soul and helps me connect with the self that I hide from the public. It's a place to renew and be authentic and I work on taking that authenticity to the real world. People come to camp assuming that they will express their authentic selves. We expect them to be authentic and this provides a culture that is quite unusual from the outside world.

Pushing personal edges and trying on new ways of being led some participants to profound insights, growth and empowerment. Participants described the rewards of the transformation as rebirth, primal healing, self-love, integrity and an overall sense of wholeness and well-being. As will be discussed next, such personal transformation is considered both a parallel and a prerequisite for social transformation. Indeed, Banshee described the connection:

> I appreciate a week of living in community as I wish my communities out in the world were. Camp contributes to my daily life by giving me a deep experience that I continue to explore once I get home. It shows me another way I might live, another way our world might be. It is far more free and edgy than my day-to-day life. It's a chance to practice and carry that back out into the world.

(Re)crafting the world: witch camp as social transformation

In talking about social change and activism, many respondents, whether or not they identified as activists, referred to the idea of creating change in the world by making change in the self or by living one's life as an enactment of the vision. Further, they saw a clear connection between their experience as witches and witch camp participants in that enactment. Jax referred to:

> the old definition of the word Witch, which is to bend and shape. I like that image of crafting my life and crafting the world around me. I'm intentionally focusing my spiritual energy internally because I want to grow into a person that is healthier and more stable and well-balanced.

Sig said:

> It's a really powerful activist thing to do to live your values, at home, not just at camp. Most of the sorting out of personal values happens at witch camp then I take them home and my activism is trying to embody that. Activism that comes from a place of alignment is going to be more effective. Creating change has the potential for conflict and it's really easy to get into power games and react. If your activism is from a place of self-love and being grounded in your values, aligned within yourself and aligned in your world, you're less likely to get pulled off balance and your activism is going to be effective.

Like many study participants, Banshee was reluctant to identify as an activist:

> I don't believe I am an activist in the way most in Reclaiming define activist. I work to change the world by changing myself. I use Magic to enlist the power, energy and support of my subconscious, with the intent to change the world for the better. For a long time, I only worked on changing myself but I didn't feel healthy or experienced enough to exert my will to change the world. Witch camp made me see that differently. Now I create experiences that let others step into growth and change.

Likewise, Rosey said:

> I'm not sure I'd call myself an activist. I have trouble with that really go-get-em radical kind of energy. I'm well acquainted with some of those 'Capital A' Activist Witches and I deeply respect them but it's not the method I choose. I went to an activism-oriented Reclaiming ritual just before a political protest a few years ago. I just did not like the ritual or the energy. It was angry and seemed focussed on building a frenzy of opposing energy and I thought that some of the people were taking themselves too seriously. I see what they are trying to accomplish and I hope to support that in other ways. I love and respect that, at camps, people are very serious about wanting to use their personal power and group power and their activities to make the world a more just place. I try to think carefully about what we do at camp and what kind of values I can integrate into my life and I try to model honesty and

tolerance and influence other people, and work on what I do with my garbage. I try not to be consumerist or participate in what is destructive and unjust in the culture.

Rocky stated that he is not an activist:

Except maybe in how I live my life. Activist makes me think of street activists but I understand that you can redefine it. There is no part of my life that I'm not willing to tell my truth in and that is the extent of my activism. For me, that is enough to change the world. It is a better way than marching downtown.

Similarly, Tree was an activist, but only in that she was:

just living the dream, I guess, by role modeling. I farm the front lawn of my house. I'm not an overt activist though. I teach with an environmental ethic but I don't define that as activism.

Gwin considered the role of witch camp in her activism:

I am living out the change I want to see in the world, namely a return to sustainable agriculture and to medicine as something practiced by everyone. Witch camp plays a role in my activism in that it infuses my life with energy to keep on doing what I'm doing. And puts me, for a week, among people who are excited about it and appreciate it.

It was Hecate's opinion that witch camps are activism:

Radically trying to embody stewardship of the land, and the teaching that happens at places like this, it verges on activism. It's empowering and it pushes you to want to carry that out in other places.

Lupina said camp prevented her from burning out as an activist, 'I am involved locally as an activist and camp feeds my activist soul. I learn new methods and it prevents burnout for me'. Camp provided Edie with, 'awareness on political issues through discussion with other campers'. She said that she had seen people, 'commit to big actions and causes because of camp'.

Jizak pondered the usefulness of witch camps being isolated from the mundane world, but valued networking and education:

I sometimes wonder if the experience of camp is valuable outside of the pleasure I get from it while I'm there. Would I be better served focusing on bringing my Magical work into the world in a way less separated from the everyday world? I love that there is space for my value of activism and of living consciously. Some campers are less interested in activism, and there is room for divergent opinions. I am an activist and I have participated in organizing and being at street actions, and I strive to make the world better through challenging some of the current socio-political structures. Witch camp provides me a place to talk about activism with others openly and freely with a common language. Witch camp also provides me with skills that help me in my activism, such as grounding, setting clear intentions, singing and dancing as ways of joyfully protesting. And the camp experience is so intense that I reflect on it throughout the year afterwards and it tends to feed my work year round.

Zevon was an activist in that she liked, 'to get involved with changing injustice. Witch camp reminds me of the sacredness of Nature and creates in me a desire to do environmental work'. Nanny said that witch camp supported the formal and informal activism that she had been doing:

My activism shows up in the way that I'm a therapist. Just the whole political context that I bring to helping people understand their personal angst of the moment. If you are anxious, well, the planet is going to hell in a hand basket so of course you're anxious. Sensitive people carry the anxiety of the culture. I bring a political analysis to all my work. I do that in the way I lead a service for the Unitarians, in the way I'm part of ritual; my activism doesn't have a box.

Shechi also identified as an activist, having been involved for over 30 years in peace activism, Palestinian-Arab issues, women's issues, immigration and gay and lesbian issues:

At witch camp, people value activism and you don't have to apologize for going to a demonstration. I'm one of two faculty in the entire university who goes to any kind of political demonstration. I will leave class to attend a rally. Other faculty have made negative comments about that. Witch camp informs my activism. I bring what I learn here back to my activism.

Soleil credited camps for her activism and involvement in the local food movement. She also said they made her more sensitive about how energy affected groups in street actions. She told a story about a rally to mark the day that the Iraq war began:

I went first to a spiritual vigil and then to the rally. The vigil was very powerful and I liked the energy. The language didn't match my spirituality but it was still about social and eco-responsibility and mourning the lack of social responsibility. There was song and a spiritual kind of energy. Then I went to the ritual. It was all angry slogans being yelled on megaphones. Through camp, I've learned how the energy you put forth changes things. If the rally had singing or some positive note, it would have been more effective. There was too much anger.

Sequoia said that she:

honestly never contemplated the link between camp and her activism. I see a link between my Reclaiming identity as a whole and my activism, but I don't know that the link is with camp. Camp has an effect on the form of my activism, but not its existence.

For Sequoia, being a Witch was:

to be a maker of Magic, an agent of both preservation and change. There are no observers at Witch camp. You are a participant and co-creator from the moment you enter the space and this may have led me to more active activism; where I used to be more of a letter-writer and administrative support volunteer, now I'm that chick with the weed wrench pulling up the buckthorn, or making a hat to donate to the local shelter, or riding my bike to make myself an example of its viability as a mode of transportation.

Rosey said that something she loves about witch camp was that, 'people are very serious about wanting to use their personal power and collective power and their own activities to make the world a more just place'. Pye said that when camp ended:

there is still connection, a sense of a bigger community, the sense of the spider web and the invisible connections holding the energy of whatever vision we've come up with here. I have comfort in knowing that I have a bigger connection out there holding the vision.

Participants were active in a variety of environmental and social justice issues both formally and informally, and they considered activism to include everyday activities related to food production and consumption, relationship to nature, work practice, philanthropy, art, public mourning and embodiment of values, particularly that of non-violence. As such, camp was an antidote, a container providing a sense of community and self-reflection, where one's personal growth and place in a collective could be positively experienced and harnessed. Also noted was the contribution of witch campers to bringing peace, playfulness and groundedness with the intention to offset what they saw as angry, violent protest.

Discussion

Magical activism

Magical activism is an overarching theme of this paper, which is braided together by the themes of building safe spaces where one can enact personal and social transformation while illuminating the spiritual component of the experience. During the early stages of data analysis, the notion of magical activism became evident and so was discussed with participants in additional interviews. Many participants thought it described their experiences of witch camp and witch culture well. Further, for many participants, merely calling oneself a Witch was a form of activism. According to Maebon, 'just being involved in an Earth-based religion is activism. It informs my sense of politics and being involved and participatory in the world at large'. Although she disagreed with some of the ways that people used activism to enact change in society, she valued witch camp as an:

> opportunity to reconnect with people who blend spirituality and activism. The rituals are well thought out and thought provoking. Camp brings together many people with alternative lifestyles and choices of political process and activism. I benefit to know that there are those who continue the work of challenging the status quo and who have energy and hope for the future. Camp is a place to express the political that is not one of violence. I believe the work done has an effect energetically and changes do come about. I consider myself an activist presently working within the system. Witch camp keeps me in touch with those on the edge. Keeping an open mind and being aware of all the expressions of spirituality and social activism helps me to be open and understanding and reminds me of the many solutions to be expressed.

Hailey said:

> If there is anything that is going to be effective about dancing around the fire and raising a cone of power or energy to create change, it's going to be changing the consciousness of the participants of that ritual. After that ritual, they then engage the world in a way that manifests the intention that was laid into the subconscious mind during the ritual.

A common ritual invocation when creating sacred space, or casting the circle, includes the words, "what happens between the worlds, changes all the world", indicating the belief that the intention or transformation energized in the sacred space of ritual (between the worlds) will also change the everyday, mundane world. Jax and Shechi talked about ritual as a time and place to envision change in the world:

> We do ritual and visualize the way that we'd like to see the world. We put into place a formal ritual that is meant to send energy out into the world, to hopefully affect some change that we'd like to see happen. (Jax)

> In creating ritual, we make stuff up that we'd like to see happen. It's a place where we get to articulate and name the way we want it to be. (Shechi)

Within the container, the sacred space, of witch camp, participants experienced relief from the norms and expectations of the dominant culture and described a sense of safety and community with the like-minded and like-hearted. Providing a shield from everyday life in the ordinary reality of the mainstream, camp offered spiritual retreat and restoration; enabling resistance to the norms and roles of traditional, patriarchal spirituality and society. The celebration of nature and Goddess as sacred in a feminist eco-spiritual community of affirmation created a culture where one could envision and embody alternatives in line with personal, spiritual and political beliefs. The notion of magical activism captures the ways witch camps and witch culture both affirm and prefigure alternatives and, perhaps most importantly, highlights the role of leisure, shaped by spiritually informed activism, in crafting a better world.

Affirming alternatives

This paper builds on research identifying the importance of alternative community and culture for affirming positive individual identity (Magliocco 2004; Murphy 1999; Salomonsen 2002). For study participants, witch camp provided an antidote to the sense of alienation they experienced in mainstream culture and provided an escape where they found sustenance, restoration and affirmation. Moreover the experience was described by some as a 'mirror' where participants could see themselves as the norm without the ugly reflections they experienced in the dominant culture. Participants felt the affirmation of their spirituality, values, beliefs, hopes and concerns reflected in the community. This 'mirror' perhaps provided the antidote to the process of internalizing the negative judgments of mainstream culture and provided a sense of affirmation strong enough to support both personal and social transformation. Indeed, this opportunity to develop individually seemed to build a movement towards a broader form of social transformation.

Prefiguring alternatives

Witch camp communities acted as prefigurative communities (Breines 1982; Sharpe 2008) and participants talked about camps as manifestations of a reality both different from, and also extended into, that of the mainstream. Berger (2005) theorized that Pagans attend festivals to gain a sense of spiritual community with those who share a particular worldview and to participate in a temporary prefigurative community. As prefigurative communities, camps provided an experience of community built on feminist eco-spirituality, a queer range of sexuality and sexual orientation, self-actualization, authenticity, contribution and service, environmental and social justice, activism and shared power. Separation, in community, acted as a shield from the dominant culture, through containment, belonging, contribution, shared ideologies and values, as well as the collective sharing of naturally induced altered states of consciousness.

Within the field of leisure studies, this study adds empirical evidence of the centrality of leisure for engendering collective and individual responsibility to prefigure, indeed, to build, if for a short time, a different kind of world; a world where concerns about broader social, political and environmental concerns are paramount (cf. Arai and Pedlar 2003; Mair 2002; Mair, Sumner, and Rotteau 2008; Sharpe 2008). This study aligns with these works and yet offers additional insights into the ways individuals, when they feel affirmed, safe, and in community, can extend themselves into broader areas of social transformation. Moreover, this study of witch camp, with its prefigurative intent, based in eco-spirituality, allows for a broader understanding of counter-culture or alternative cultures as well as the role of spirituality and leisure therein.

Affirming spirituality and activism

This research helps to address the need for more assessments of spirituality and leisure (Heintzman 2006; Karlis, Grafanski, and Abbas 2002) and extends our understanding beyond the standard Christian-based lens (Stodolska and Livengood 2006) by offering a glimpse into the spiritual beliefs and activism of a group that is positioned at the margins. Participants identified witch camp as a source of validation for their beliefs and their desire for change in the wider world. Comments about internalizing principles, learning to exert one's will to change the world, taking personal responsibility and the sacralisation of the earth community contributed to taking action. According to Finley (1991), feminist witchcraft teaches empowerment, personal responsibility and political efficacy and is a motivator of social action. Engaging in feminist witchcraft is a political act in itself because it challenges the patriarchal political system (Greenwood 2000). Similarly, Partridge (2005) described eco-Paganism as spiritual resistance in its rejection of patriarchal religion in favour of Goddess or Earth-based spirituality. As noted by participants, merely acknowledging one's identity as a Witch or contributing to witch camp constituted active resistance to the norm.

Conclusion

This paper contributes to the position of leisure as a dynamic force in social and political change (Mair 2002; Gilchrist and Ravenscroft 2013; Lashua 2005; Sharpe 2008; Shaw 2001). It also highlights the role of spirituality and community in social change. Through the creation of safe and sacred spaces, witch camp participants raised consciousness, fostered personal transformation and also enhanced their political and social justice efficacy. Future studies should investigate the experience of campers or other members of so-called alternative cultures, as they move between these worlds and trace their efforts to both hide and to foreground the parts of themselves that are marginalized when they are away from the support of their community. Further research is also needed to explore the tensions and challenges within this and other alternative cultures to better appreciate the extent to which these communities are also bound by social practices, rules and regulations, which may embolden but may also silence dissenters and more radical voices.

Acknowledgement

A special and heartfelt 10-fingered twinkle to study participants for being willing, open, thoughtful, smart and funny.

References

Abrahams, R. 1982. "Ordinary and Extraordinary Experience." In *Celebration: Studies in Festivity and Ritual*, edited by V. Turner. 108–135. Chicago: University of Illinois Press.

Ammerman, N. 1997. "Organized Religion in a Voluntaristic Society." *Sociology of Religion* 58 (3): 203–215. doi:10.2307/3712213.

Arai, S., and A. Pedlar. 2003. "Moving beyond Individualism in Leisure Theory: A Critical Analysis of Concepts of Community and Social Engagement." *Leisure Studies* 22 (3): 185–202. doi:10.1080/026143603200075489.

Berger, H. 2005. *Witchcraft and Magic: Contemporary North America*. Philadelphia: University of Pennsylvania Press.

Breines, W. 1982. *Community and Organization in the New Left, 1962–1968: The Great Refusal*. New Brunswick, NJ: Rutgers University Press.

Browne, K. 2007. "A Party with Politics? (Re)making LGBTQ Pride Spaces in Dublin and Brighton." *Social & Cultural Geography* 8 (1): 63–87. doi:10.1080/14649360701251817.

Calley Jones, C. 2010. "Playing at the Queer Edges." *Leisure Studies* 29 (3): 269–287. doi:10.1080/02614360903401935.

Cerny, J. 2004. "Social Change and Spirituality: Planting Seeds of Hope and Promise from Spiritual Roots." *Canadian Review of Social Policy* 54: 135–141.

Charmaz, K. 2006. *Constructing Grounded Theory: A Practical Guide through Qualitative Analysis*. Thousand Oaks, CA: SAGE.

Creswell, J. 2003. *Research Design: Qualitative, Quantitative, and Mixed Methods Approaches*. Thousand Oaks, CA: SAGE.

Cush, D. 2007. "Consumer Witchcraft: Are Teenage Witches a Creation of Commercial Interests?" *Journal of Beliefs and Values* 28 (1): 45–53. doi:10.1080/13617670701251439.

deMunck, V., and E. Sobo, eds. 1998. *Using Methods in the Field: A Practical Introduction and Casebook*. Walnut Creek, CA: AltaMira Press.

De Souza, M. 2003. "Contemporary Influences on the Spirituality of Young People: Implications for Education." *International Journal of Children's Spirituality* 8 (3): 269–279. doi:10.1080/1364436032000146539.

Eder, D., S. Staggenborg, and L. Sudderth. 1995. "The National Women's Music Festival: Collective Identity and Diversity in a Lesbian-feminist Community." *Journal of Contemporary Ethnography* 23 (4): 485–515. doi:10.1177/089124195023004004.

Falassi, A. 1967. "Festival: Definition and Morphology." In *Time Out of Time: Essays on the Festival*, edited by A. Falassi, 1–10. Albuquerque: University of New Mexico Press.

Finley, N. J. 1991. "Political Activism and Feminist Spirituality." *Sociological Analysis* 52 (4): 349–362. doi:10.2307/3710851.

Freire, P. 1970. *Pedagogy of the Oppressed*. New York: Continuum.

Gilchrist, P., and N. Ravenscroft. 2013. "Space Hijacking and the Anarcho-politics of Leisure." *Leisure Studies* 32 (1): 49–68. doi:10.1080/02614367.2012.680069.

Glesne, C., and A. Peshkin. 1992. *Becoming Qualitative Researchers: An Introduction*. White Plains, NY: Longman.

Greenwood, S. 2000. *Magic, Witchcraft, and the Otherworld: An Anthropology*. New York: Berg.

Heintzman, P. 2006. "Listening for a Leisure Remix in Ancient Israel and Early Christianity." *Leisure Sciences* 28 (5): 431–435. doi:10.1080/01490400600851247.

Hemingway, J. L. 1999. "Critique and Emancipation: Toward a Critical Theory of Leisure. In *Leisure Studies: Prospects for the 21st Century*, edited by E. L. Jackson and T. L. Burton. State College, PA: Venture.

Holloway, J. 2003. "Make-believe: Spiritual Practice, Embodiment, and Sacred Space." *Environment and Planning A* 35 (11): 1961–1974. doi:10.1068/a3586.

Hume, L. 1997. *Witchcraft and Paganism in Australia*. Carlton South: Melbourne University Press.

Jackson, P. 1992. "The Politics of the Streets: A Geography of Caribana." *Political Geography* 11 (2): 130–151. doi:10.1016/0962-6298(92)90045-U.

Karlis, G., S. Grafanski, and J. Abbas. 2002. "Leisure and Spirituality: A Theoretical Model." *Society and Leisure* 25 (1): 205–214.

Kong, L. 2001. "Mapping 'New' Geographies of Religion: Politics and Poetics in Modernity." *Progress in Human Geography* 25 (2): 211–233. doi:10.1191/030913201678580485.

Lashua, B. D. 2005. "Leisure, Civil Disobedience, and the History of Low Power FM (LPFM) Radio." *Leisure* [Loisir] 29 (1): 27–48. doi:10.1080/14927713.2005.9651322.

Magliocco, S. 2004. *Witching Culture: Folklore and Neo-Paganism in America.* Philadelphia: University of Pennsylvania Press.

Mair, H. 2002. "Civil Leisure? Exploring the Relationship between Leisure, Activism and Social Change." *Leisure* [Loisir] 27 (3/4): 213–237. doi:10.1080/14927713.2002.9651304.

Mair, H., J. Sumner, and L. Rotteau. 2008. "The Politics of Eating: Food Practices as Critically Reflexive Leisure." *Leisure* [Loisir] 32 (2): 379–405. doi:10.1080/14927713.2008.9651415.

Morris, B. 2005. "Negotiating Lesbian Worlds: The Festival Communities." *Journal of Lesbian Studies* 9 (1/2): 55–62. doi:10.1300/J155v09n01_05.

Murphy, B. K. 1999. *Transforming Ourselves; Transforming the World: An Open Conspiracy for Social Change.* Halifax: Fernwood.

Partridge, C. 2005. *The Re-enchantment of the West: Alternative Spiritualties, Sacralization, Popular Culture, and Occulture* (Vol. 2). New York: T & T Clark International.

Pike, S. 2001. *Earthly Bodies, Magical Selves: Contemporary Pagans and the Search for Community.* Berkley: University of California Press.

Rojek, C., S. M. Shaw, and A. J. Veal. 2006. "Introduction: Process and Content." In *A Handbook of Leisure Studies*, edited by C. Rojek, S. M. Shaw, and A. J. Veal, 1–24. New York: Palgrave MacMillan.

Rountree, K. 2004. *Embracing the Witch and the Goddess: Feminist Ritual Makers in New Zealand.* London: Routledge.

Salomonsen, J. 2002. *Enchanted Feminism: The Reclaiming Witches of San Francisco.* New York: Routledge.

Shaw, S. 2001. "Conceptualizing Resistance: Women's Leisure as Political Practice." *Journal of Leisure Research* 33 (2): 186–201.

Shaw, S. 2004. "At the Water's Edge: An Ecologically Inspired Methodology." In *Researching Paganisms*, edited by J. Blain, D. Ezzy, and G. Harvey, 131–145. Toronto, ON: AltaMira Press.

Sharpe, E. K. 2008. "Festivals and Social Change: Intersections of Pleasure and Politics at a Community Music Festival." *Leisure Sciences* 30 (3): 217–234. doi:10.1080/01490400802017324.

Starhawk. 2011. *The Empowerment Manual: A Guide for Collaborative Groups.* Gabriola Island, BC: New Society.

Stodolska, M., and J. Livengood. 2006. "The Influence of Religion on the Leisure Behaviour of Immigrant Muslims in the United States." *Journal of Leisure Research* 38 (3): 293–320.

Turner, V. 1982. "Introduction." In *Celebration: Studies in Festivity and Ritual*, edited by V. Turner, 11–30. Chicago: University of Illinois Press.

Van Schyndel Kasper, D. 2008. "Redefining Community in the Ecovillage." *Human Ecology Review* 15 (1): 12–24.

Waterman, S. 1998. "Carnivals for Elites? The Cultural Politics of Arts Festivals." *Progress in Human Geography* 22 (1): 54–74. doi:10.1191/030913298672233886.

Wolf. 2006. "The Allure of WitchCamp." *Witchvox Website*: Articles/Essays from Pagans, Article 10891, VoxAcct 295487. Accessed December 31, 2009. http://www.witchvox.com/.

Does Bear do it for you? Gen-Y gappers and alternative tourism

Jonathan Joseph and Stephen L. Wearing

Management Discipline Group, UTS Business School, University of Technology Sydney, Sydney, NSW, Australia

Popular culture and travel are both major points of interest within the realm of leisure in contemporary consumer society. Respectively, they are both highly contentious and diverse fields. This paper explores the more specific areas of popular culture celebrities and alternative tourism in an effort to examine the influence that popular culture and travel engagements have on a segment of Generation Y (Gen-Y) – the gappers. These two areas of leisure activity shape social and cultural norms and influence the construction of self-identity amongst this generation. The aim of this exploratory research is to highlight some areas where popular culture and alternative tourism can be valued as constructive factors influencing a Gen-Y group. The theory of planned behaviour acted as a framework and was used to identify the influence that popular culture celebrity 'Bear' Grylls and his TV show *Man vs. Wild* had on the alternative tourism engagements of the Gen-Y gappers.

Introduction

This paper explores the influence that popular culture has on the travel engagements of Generation Y (Gen-Y) gappers. It then goes on to examine how popular culture and alternative travel might shape social and cultural norms as well as influence the construction of self-identity. The aim of the paper is to highlight some areas where popular culture and alternative tourism can be valued as constructive factors influencing a Gen-Y group. A case study of Edward 'Bear' Grylls and his TV show *Man vs. Wild* was used to explore the impacts of alternative tourism engagements on the Gen-Y gappers. It then looked to understand whether these travel engagements had an influence over their subsequent lifestyles. Studying how popular culture celebrities and alternative tourism engagements impacted the beliefs, attitudes, motivations and behaviours of a Gen-Y subgroup – the gappers – was a main focus. The selection of popular culture figure Edward 'Bear' Grylls, as an example for this research, stems from his status as 'one of the world's most recognised faces of survival and outdoor adventure' (Bear Grylls Ventures 2013).

In this paper, the idea of popular culture was further refined in order to focus on the celebrity phenomenon. Popular culture was examined to see how it might reinforce and legitimise social and cultural norms and provide social comfort and shared meaning through consumption. Additionally, it investigated how opportunities for self-expression, self-enhancement and the legitimisation of a diverse range of experiences might be enabled. The concept of a gap year, which is seen as a popular option for travel amongst the youth tourism market (Lyons and Wearing 2011), refined the ideas expressed above. This considered how alternative tourism can be deemed as a way to build the participants identity, learn to be self-sufficient and reliant, develop their values and ambitions, and stimulate personal growth.

Popular culture plays a pivotal role in shaping the content people consume. This content may include tangible products, experiences, information or even knowledge. Popular culture celebrities, particularly in contemporary society, often come under criticism for their superficiality. This research challenged this commonly held perception of popular culture by unveiling a more authentic side. Using what Krieken terms a celebrity spectrum or a 'celebrity effect', popular culture is presented as a part of our institutionalised social lives rather than something that is taboo or mysterious (2012, 7). The notion of celebrities as vicarious role models was also examined (Bush, Martin, and Bush 2004). As Gen-Y tends to see celebrities as realistic representations of themselves or of the general public, they are able to connect with them more so than previous generations do (Morton 2002).

Any content that an individual or group continually interacts with or consumes may shape self-identity (McDonald and Wearing 2013), knowledge, motivations, beliefs, attitudes and behaviours (Noble, Haytko, and Phillips 2009). However, research on awareness to action conversion is relatively ambiguous across the disciplines of consumer culture (Noble, Haytko, and Phillips 2009) and the tourism industry (Wearing and Neil 2009). To provide framework, the theory of planned behaviour (TPB) (Ajzen 1985, 1991) was used to identify the influence that the popular culture celebrity 'Bear' Grylls (as he is commonly known) and his TV show *Man vs. Wild* had on the alternative tourism engagements of the Gen-Y gappers being studied.

As young people are significant contributors to the international tourism market, research on alternative youth tourism is growing (Richards and Wilson 2005). By focusing on alternative tourism, this paper investigated the potential outcomes for those subjects that engage in a more altruistic travel experience.

Central to this research is the following rationale:

> The most profound satisfactions are to be found in living a life in accord with the natural world, exercising the human capacity for friendship and altruism, engaging in creative and purposeful activity, and experiencing an allegiance to one's origins ... But it is insufficient such a message; one has to experience it to know that things are so. (Michael King 1999, pp. 240 cited in Wattchow and Brown 2011)

The intention of the study was to develop a better understanding of how Gen-Y gappers relate to popular culture and travel. This was realised in terms of consumption motivations and identity creation amongst the gapper participants.

Literature review

Gen-Y is a highly diverse and sophisticated generation. Social researcher Mark McCrindle (2009) defines Gen-Ys as those born between 1980 and 1994. For this generation, financial commitments are disregarded, recreational pursuits are predominantly socially orientated and media, globalisation, travel, cultural diversity and environmentalism have shaped their beliefs, attitudes and lifestyles (McCrindle 2002; Morton 2002; Patterson 2007; Wolburg and Pokrywczynski 2001; Shearer 2002). According to Williamson (2008), Gen-Ys are characterised as being optimistic, confident, sociable, strong in morals, having a sense of civic duty, motivated by inspiring leadership and are actively seeking for continuous learning through creativity and innovation. There are 4.2 million Gen-Ys in Australia, comprising 20% of the nation's population (McCrindle 2009). In the USA alone, there are around 80 million Gen-Ys. They make up about 25% of the American population (Escalera 2012).

Gen-Ys have grown up in a consumer orientated society (Bush, Martin, and Bush 2004; Noble, Haytko, and Phillips 2009; Wearing, McDonald, and Wearing 2013). They have transformed the consumer market through their tremendous spending power as they have more disposable money than any other group in history (Morton 2002). Gen-Y currently represents the largest consumer group in U S History (Morton 2002) with an average annual spending of US$200 billion (Kerwin 2012). Consequently, they are one of the most watched generations by the media in recent history. This has heavily influenced the way that information and content are communicated to them (Howe and Strauss 2000). The diversity and spread of popular culture content, technological developments, politics, mass marketing and the liberalisation of global economies drive these trends. Lcd by neoliberal western economies, these factors significantly contribute to the aspirations and opinions of Gen-Y (McCrindle 2002, 2009; Morton 2002). Cowen (2008) identifies younger people as having an obsession with purchasing the latest releases, creative culture and social experiences. This understanding of consumer society stems from the interdisciplinary field of consumer culture, which embodies the economic, cultural, social and institutional processes that drive the need to consume or possess something of value (Featherstone 2001; Lury 1996; Lury 2011; Stebbins 2009; Wearing, McDonald, and Wearing 2013).

All these considerations lead to the view that Gen-Y is heavily influenced by contemporary popular culture (Cowen 2008; McCrindle 2002), travel (Lyons et al. 2012; Richards and Wilson 2004), new media (Bull et al. 2008; Prensky 2001), global citizenship (McCrindle 2009), creative culture and multi-faceted experiences (Cowen 2008; Williamson 2008). Despite having a better understanding of the characteristics that commonly define Gen-Y, a great deal is still unknown about the motivations behind their consumerist behaviours (Noble, Haytko, and Phillips 2009).

Popular culture

Studying popular culture in the contemporary sense is important as it plays a multi-dimensional, pervasive and covert role in reinforcing people's beliefs and behaviours through its consumption (Sellnow 2010). Popular culture has empowering and disempowering attributes due to its 'persuasive power to shape beliefs and behaviours' (Sellnow 2010, 5). Popular culture seeks to entertain the audience, generate stimuli that people can personally or collectively relate to and provide novelty that is not overwhelming.

Harrington and Bielby (2001) identify popular culture as works that are produced for consumption, where the objects and content are often being created by the people themselves. Popular culture is comprised of everyday artifacts, actions and events, such as movies, television shows, music, sports, print media and literature. These aspects influence the audiences' beliefs and behaviours (Sellnow 2010). Popular culture creates points of identification amongst individuals and groups (Mankekar 2001) and it also re-enforces how people should behave (Sellnow 2010). Similarly, Mankekar (2001) recognises popular culture as a domain that shapes our sense of self and our identity amongst large groups of people. It also creates points of identification amongst groups within a community.

In order to conceptualise the contemporary nature of popular culture, consumer culture theories were examined. Featherstone highlights how the contemporary focus of consumption impacts consumer culture far 'beyond the negative evaluation of consumer pleasures inherited from mass culture theory' (2007, 42). This undermines the view that mass-produced products are inherently alien in nature and that they can condition the consumer's response (Campbell 2005). Major technological and socio-economic changes in global politics and the dynamic nature of postmodern leisure have radically shifted consumer behaviours (Lury 1996). Modifications in societal preferences since the mid–late twentieth century have birthed a society-led compulsion to acquire goods. This tendency to consume highly accessible goods and services is driven by the consumer society (Wearing, McDonald, and Wearing 2013). This stems from the interdisciplinary field of consumer culture, which embodies the economic, cultural, social and institutional processes that drive the need to consume or possess something of value (Featherstone 2001; Lury 1996; Lury 2011; Stebbins 2009; Wearing, McDonald, and Wearing 2013). Subsequently, consumer culture has built on the notion of cultural and social norms and the legitimisation of self-identity through the consumption of goods and services (Baudrillard [1970] 1998).

A collectivistic view considers the attainment of goods and services as important and valuable in its own right (Ritzer 2007). In addition, Kacen and Lee (2002) identify consumer culture as forms of collectivism and social norms. Creators of popular culture view themselves as the architects of signs and symbols appropriate to their audiences and to themselves (Lipsitz 2001). Amongst Gen-Y, this enables a sense of belonging to a cultural phenomenon (Cowen 2008; Noble, Haytko, and Phillips 2009). This is where people are 'often motivated by norms and duties imposed by the in-group' and subsequently moderate their consumption behaviours in order to emphasise their connectedness within the group' (Kacen and Lee 2002, 165). The notion of consumption extends further than the basic attainment and exchange of goods and services (Stebbins 2009). As a type of cultural resource or possession, consumer culture legitimises self-identity (Lury 1996). This reflects the 'consumer socialisation' concept. As discussed by Bush, Martin, and Bush (2004), consumer socialisation emphasises the varied ways by which young people acquire norms, knowledge, attitudes, motivations and behaviours. Additionally, Campbell (2005) refers to a new way of categorising consumers. The term 'craft consumers' goes beyond the notion of consuming for lifestyle and identity as it focuses on consumer's need to engage in creative acts of self-expression. In this case, consumers already have a clear sense of identity and distinct modes of consuming.

According to Mankekar (2001), popular culture is the culture of the masses, with neoliberalism and the consumer society enabling greater accessibility. This has been propelled by the nature of postmodern leisure, globalisation (McCrindle 2002) and technological changes in communication (Lim, Chou, and Melewar 2008; Nusair et al. 2013) which have accelerated the convergence of popular culture within Gen-Y. As it is a continual point of reference to consumerism and consumer society, popular culture plays an important role in representing and exposing the public to itself. In doing so, it constitutes the process of making sense of the world around us and our interaction with others (Mankekar 2001).

Individuals engage with media as critical and creative consumers (Dunlap and Johnson 2013; Johnson, Richmond, and Kivel 2008; Kivel and Johnson 2009). Popular culture, for instance through film and television, acts as an agent of social control and change (Slocum 2000 cited in Beeton 2006, 6). Popular media can also influence travel behaviours and activities by developing or reinforcing specific images through people and destinations (Beeton 2006). A postmodernist view assumes that symbolic images, as distilled by popular culture, dominate the fabric of our social lives (McRobbie 1994). Kellner (1991) looks at television as an entertainment medium that produces familiar narratives for consumers. Moreover, Cowen believes that by consuming culture, Gen-Y is 'consuming this idea of connection' (2008, 263). This is because social norms enforce a sense of inclusion or exclusion. In fact, Kellner argues that 'mass-media culture play key roles in the structuring of contemporary identity' (1991, 148). In addition, media consumption is an influential medium by which individuals confront social norms and cultural values (Dunlap and Johnson 2013).

Contemporary mass media has brought people together without them ever really knowing each other (Lipsitz 2001). For example, new media and technology have changed the way consumers interact with the travel industry. By embracing interactive forms of online media such as review sites, social networks and travel blogs, users are allowed to be more socially connected when evaluating travel decisions (Nusair et al. 2013). Compared to traditional marketing approaches, these new forms of media, for instance film, television and online mechanisms, arc powerful marketing tools in reaching a larger target audience (Beeton 2005; Hudson, Wang, and Gill 2011; Nusair et al. 2013).

Film-induced tourism can be defined as when a 'tourist visits to a destination or attraction as a result of the destination being featured' through various media sources including, television, video, DVD or the cinema screen (Hudson and Ritchie 2006, 256). Existing literature into media induced tourism draws attention to the overall phenomenon of communication through media. Interestingly, tourism as stimulated by popular culture media in not a new occurrence (Lundberg and Lexhagen 2012). Audiences model their behaviours and attitudes on television and media content (Kellner 1991). According to Frost (2009), the connection that is created between the viewer and the events, places and characters portrayed in the media stimulus (Kim and Richardson 2003; Müller 2006) is based on the notion of a constructed reality. Both authentic and fictitious accounts create emotional ties with the audience (Frost 2009). Visual media, for instance television programs and film, plays an important role in inducing tourism (Beeton 2006). Wolburg and Pokrywczynski (2001) propose that new media strategies should incorporate characters from TV shows, film stars and other personalities who are highly identifiable with Gen-Y as a way to harness a more transparent convergence of consumer self-identity and perceived brand identity. According to Hudson and Ritchie (2006), films can have a powerful impact on a destination image. However, as a complex and dynamic concept, further research is required on film tourism and its psychological and behavioural influences on the audience.

Gen-Y is increasingly engrossed by the lives of popular culture celebrities (Bush, Martin, and Bush 2004; McCrindle 2009; Morton 2002; Noble, Haytko, and Phillips 2009). When considering celebrities, this paper questioned the assumption of superficiality. This is because this assumption prevents an understanding of the impact that celebrities or personalities have on society (Celebrity Society 2012). Vicarious role models, such as sports stars, actors, political figures, philanthropists and motivational speakers, influence individuals in terms of their 'heroic' qualities (Bauman 2005; Shuart 2007). As celebrities are a prominent form of popular culture, the example of 'Bear' Grylls was used to highlight the way certain celebrities can be seen as role models with values that positively influence the audience. Understanding Gen-Y gappers from this perspective emphasised their role as contemporary consumers and also drew attention to the way that popular culture shapes individual and collective identities.

Identity, image and culture, as social constructs, are harnessed by popular media to cultivate the motivations and behaviours of young people (Beeton 2006; Bush, Martin, and Bush 2004). Beeton (2006) considers the culture of fame as a 'cult of celebrity', which has exponentially grown though popular culture. Celebrity society tends to be overlooked as a 'serious topic' by the social sciences (Krieken 2012, 12). However, Krieken (2012) views the notion of the 'cult of celebrity' as being limited. Assessing celebrities as cult objects, obsessions or superficial figures often impedes a more thorough and inclusive understanding of the phenomenon being studied. Krieken's (2012) concept of a 'celebrity society' means that more attention is paid to the social structuring of the celebrity and the way they are assigned, distributed, organised and responded to as a form of institutionalised social life. Krieken (2012) characterises celebrities by their capacity to attract attention (positive or negative), according to their desire to generate some benefit from their infamy. They often allow for some degree of identification amongst their audience, particularly if they have a distinctive narrative to their celebrity status or quality.

Interestingly, Shuart's (2007) study of college-aged students found that the heroic qualities of the endorser were the strongest contributors in consumer motivation and purchase intent. The commonly held opposition between the 'celebrity' and 'hero' status amongst figures in society was, therefore, questioned (Bauman 2005). Celebrities are often labelled as superficial creations of the media, whilst the hero is defined by his or her achievements (Boorstin 1962; Krieken 2012). However, in many respects, the convergence of the two terms, celebrity and hero, is more prevalent in modern society. In this case, Krieken aims to reflect on the 'significance of celebrity for our everyday life, our sense of self, and relations of status, recognition and power' (2012, 1–2). This is particularly relevant when the notion of hero and celebrity exists alongside each other.

In contemporary society, the brands and messages communicated by 'Bear' Grylls, as a notable and inspirational public figure (Bear Grylls Ventures 2013; Grylls 2011), serve to juxtapose the brands associated with more contentious celebrities, such as Paris Hilton, Kim Kardashian, Kate Moss, Charlie Sheen and Tiger Woods (Celebrity Society 2012). This comparison makes it possible to de-construct the commonly held assumption that celebrities always have a negative influence on Gen-Y and the public as a whole.

This study examined the influence that 'Bear' Grylls and his former Emmy nominated TV show *Man vs. Wild*[1] had on Gen-Y gappers. As such, it explored the possible ways that popular culture content affected the participants of the study on which this paper is based. Throughout his show, the charismatic and adventurous Britain, 'Bear' Grylls hosted and narrated conveyed themes of adventure in the wilderness and experience seeking in the natural environment. The personal challenges and continuous search for self-identity in the outdoors resonate with the audience (Discovery Channel 2013; IMDb 2013). The show saw 'Bear' Grylls navigate some of the most remote and harshest locations in the world. For instance, he trekked across the Australian outback, the jungles of Costa Rica, the frozen wilderness of Iceland, the swaps of the Florida Everglades and the ravines in the Alps (Discovery Channel 2013; IMDb 2013).

'Bear' Grylls experienced cold conditions, raging waters, deserts, jungles, swamps and mountainous topographies in order to show the audience how to brave the elements. As he travelled through these destinations with a small production team, he shared survival strategies (Discovery Channel Australia 2013). As such, his show was a hybrid of entertainment, informative and educational genres. Impressively, the program became the number one cable show in America, reaching a global audience of over 1.2 billion in over 200 countries. The show spanned over 7 seasons and over 60 episodes (IMDb 2013).

'Bear' Grylls has created a global following through his work as an adventurer, writer, television host, scout leader and motivational figure (Bear Grylls Ventures 2013). He has authored 11 books, 4 of them being concerned with teenage survival skills. His autobiography, *Mud, Sweat and Tears*, stayed at number one on the *Sunday Times* best seller list in the UK for nine weeks. In testament to his services, 'Bear' Grylls was appointed Chief Scout to 28 million scouts worldwide and was awarded an honorary commission as a Lieutenant-Commander in the Royal Navy (Bear Grylls Ventures 2013). According to 'Bear' Grylls, this achievement was a very proud moment in his life (Grylls 2011). He also embraces his position as a role model for many young people around the world, endeavouring to help them realise their dreams and ultimately benefit the global community (Grylls 2011).

Popular culture and consumerism are features of everyday life (Harrington and Bielby 2001; Lury 1996; Mankekar 2001; Sellnow 2010). In contemporary society, our insatiable desire to consume is driven by popular culture and its various organs. These organs include products and services, such as media, film, television, celebrities, entertainment, events and literature. As a consequence of modernity, identities have become unstable and fragile with less substance and coherence (Kellner 1991). In response to such instability, consumption patterns have become more complex. As such, consumption is considered by Campbell to be an 'activity in which individuals not merely exercise control over the consumption process, but also bring skill, knowledge, judgement, love and passion to their consuming' (2005, 27). Exploring the notion of celebrity beyond its surface value conceptualises its meaning and purpose as part of our social, economic, political and cultural lives (Krieken 2012). Moreover, consideration should be given to the way the everyday person consumes popular culture content and messages and the way this shapes their motivations, values and attitudes.

Travel experiences

In order to refine the focus of the travel component of the study on which this paper is based, alternative tourism within the context of youth tourism was examined. Amongst Gen-Y gappers, alternative tourism has become a popular travel option (Lyons et al. 2012; Lyons and Wearing 2011). Mieczkowski (1995) explains the relationship between alternative tourism and conventional mass tourism. Alternative tourism is represented as a broad category that contains multiple forms that are alternatives to mass tourism (Wearing and Neil 2009). During the 1970s and 1980s, 'new' forms of tourism began to challenge the appeal of conventional mass tourism (Pearce 1994). These particular travel experiences focussed on specific attractions, such as a cultural location, a particular landscape or on groups of people (Dearden and Harron 1992). They are also essentially small scale, low density, dispersed in non-urban areas and cater to special interest groups (Wearing and Neil 2009).

In recent decades, the youth travel market has grown into a considerable tourism segment. One of the major reasons for the growth in youth travel is due to the popularity and appeal of a gap year. A gap year is when a person delays further education or employment in order to travel, whilst a 'gapper' is a person who partakes in a gap year (Millington 2005). This practice was first popularised in the UK during the 1950s, thereafter spreading across to the USA, Australia and New Zealand (Lyons et al. 2012). Historically, the origins of gap year travel are linked to the backpacker experience.

Gap year travel encapsulates a wide range of travel experiences that are aimed at being more personalised and authentic (Lyons and Wearing 2011). Taking a gap year has been commonly viewed as a rite of passage for young people. This, however, does not preclude the growing interest amongst the older demographics, as they value it as a form of escapism (Hirschorn and Hefferon 2013). Attempting to define the over 50-year-old phenomenon can be quite difficult due to the variety of travel options available, demographic variations and diverse travel motivations (Jones 2004).

A gap year encapsulates a range of travel experiences that can further be segmented into forms of niche tourism (Novelli 2005). These categories can include alternative tourism, organised mass travel, gastronomic and sport tourism, as well as work-related and educational travel. As alternative tourism is often interpreted as a polarised opposite and substitute for mass tourism (Weaver and Lawton 2007), the very act of defining it is relatively contentious (Higgins-Desbiolles 2008).

When analysing the practice of taking a gap year from a neoliberalist perspective, the commercialisation of travel experiences is often discussed (Simpson 2005). This often raises the notion of the professionalisation of the gap year, whereby experiences from travel help to build skills to enable young people to compete better in the market place (Simpson 2005; Lyons et al. 2012). A gap year can encourage global citizenry, broaden the mind (Simpson 2005), promote the discovery of cross-cultural experiences to help build the travellers identity (Jones 2005; Hirschorn and Hefferon 2013), autonomy (Brown 2009; Christofi and Thompson 2007), self-efficiency (Cushner and Karim 2004), time satisfaction (Elsrud 1998; Montuori and Fahim 2004) and creativity (Maddux and Galinsky 2009). It can also serve as a way to discover the self and develop interests and ambitions, values and strengths (Lyons et al. 2012).

Most Gen-Y travellers view travel as an intrinsic part of their lifestyle, though motivations vary between peer groups, destinations and travel styles (Richards and Wilson 2004). Youth travel accounts for over 20% of international tourist arrivals and is worth an estimated US$136 billion a year. This is due to the longer than average trip duration and the increasing spending power of the youth travel market (WTO 2008). Considering the variations in age groups, niche markets and travel purposes, the UNWTO (World Tourism Organisation) in consultation with the youth travel industry supports the World Youth and Student Travel Education Travel Confederation's definition of youth travel. They classify it as follows:

> Youth travel includes all independent trips for periods of less than one year by people aged 16-29 which are motivated, in part or in full, by a desire to experience other cultures, build life experience and/or benefit from formal and informal learning opportunities outside one's usual environment. (World Tourism Organisation 2008, 1)

Gap year travel, as a form of youth tourism, represents one of the most significant sectors of the tourism industry (Lyons and Wearing 2011). According to Richards and Wilson (2005), present day travellers are seeking more adventure, multi-faceted experiences and exposure to international cultures. This is due to the youth market's desire for culture, adventure, new experiences, expansive challenges and creative opportunism. Youth tourism has become an increasingly mainstream form of youth culture and has almost become a social norm.

A study undertaken in 2002 by the International Student Travel Confederation generated a greater understanding into the behaviours, motivations and activities of youth travellers (cited in Richards and Wilson 2005). The findings indicated that youth and student travellers are experience seekers, searching for culture, adventure and relaxation. In actual fact, the World Tourism Organisation (WTO) (2008) stated that the majority of young travellers feel as though they have broadened their horizons and have become more open-minded, flexible, confident and tolerant because of their travel experiences. This makes them feel more connected to the global community post-travel.

Alternative tourism, a popular component of gap year travel, is primarily focused on social, cultural and community values with a greater interaction with the natural environment and adventure (Wearing and Neil 2009). Travel that fosters these values allows for positive and worthwhile interactions and shared experiences for both the host and guest (Eadington and Smith 1994).

This is in contrast to the more commercialised and conventional forms of mass tourism where the experiences tend to be more superficial and provide a smaller contribution to the host community (Wearing and Ponting 2009). The origins of alternative tourism can be dated back to the 1960s counterculture movement that aimed to critique and reject consumer society (Lanfant and Graburn 1992). Although rather radical in many forms, this social movement acted as a catalyst for more humanistic forms of globalisation (Higgins-Desbiolles 2008). Since the 1980s, the ecotourism phenomenon has become the most optimal way to conjoin economic development with environmental sustainability (Wearing and Neil 2009).

Alternative tourism can also be seen as the overarching umbrella that encompasses a diverse range of tourism markets (Benson 2005). Alternative tourism includes such categories as 'ecotourism' (Wearing and Neil 2009), 'sustainable tourism' (Wheeller 1993), 'new tourism' (Mowforth and Munt 2003) and 'volunteer tourism' (Wearing 2001). This is because it supports ecological sustainability, conservation, environmental appreciation and community engagement, which are integral core values. Eco-trekking, for example, is thought to be low impact and offers benefits to local communities. As a form of ecotourism, it can involve travel 'to relatively undisturbed natural areas for study, enjoyment or volunteer assistance that concerns itself with the flora, fauna, geology and ecosystems of an area – as well as the people who live nearby, their needs, their culture and the relationship to the land' (Swanson 1992, 2). Another example is volunteer tourism. Despite increasing concern over its commercial development and packaging (Lyons et al. 2012; Lyons and Wearing 2011), as a rapidly growing form of ethical tourism and as a gap year option it intends to foster mutual understanding and respect (Lyons and Wearing 2008; Wearing 2001).

McDonald, Wearing, and Ponting's (2009) study on 'The Nature of Peak Experiences in Wilderness' highlights the significance of alternative tourism through a nature-oriented experience. The study looked at distinctive elements within wilderness settings that trigger peak experiences. The results showed that the aesthetic qualities of the wilderness and isolation (with individuals being removed from the pressures of people and distractions and concerns of the urban environment) were influential in the respondents' peak experiences (McDonald, Wearing, and Ponting 2009). This study also looked at whether some of the alternative travel experiences of the respondents triggered similar reflections of peak experiences. This included elements of self-discovery, personal growth, self-efficiency, discovery and a heightened awareness of global cultures.

Motivations and behaviours

Despite being an exploratory research, the paper aimed to identify the influence of popular culture and alternative travel engagements on the motivations, beliefs, attitudes and the behavioural intentions of the Gen-Y participants. The term 'motivation' is often used to describe 'what gets people going, keeps them going, and helps them finish tasks' (Pintrich 2003, 104). At a fundamental level, motivations resonate with behavioural intentions and behavioural enactments (Martin 2010). The TPB is utilised to explain the rational relationship between beliefs, attitudes, behaviours and social norms (Ajzen 1985, 1991) through the lens of popular culture and travel. In order to test the model, the theory was used to identify the influence that popular culture celebrity 'Bear' Grylls and his TV show *Man vs. Wild* had on the alternative tourism engagements of the Gen-Y gappers. This theory was only used as a framework to assist in explaining this specific phenomenon.

Motivations and cultural influences are key elements that govern Gen-Y travel behaviours (Swarbrook and Horner 2007). However, due to numerous variables (such as economic issues, culture, environmental factors, political beliefs, education, age and gender), categorising a traveller's motivations is not simple (Smed 2012). As a result, the diversity in gap year options for young people has disqualified the notion of a stereotypical traveller (Jones 2004). According to some researchers, no single theory can encompass all travel motivations. In fact, it is the heterogeneous nature of tourism itself and the complexities associated with human behaviours that makes tourism motivations highly nuanced (Bolan, Boy, and Bell 2012). According to Jones (2004), young people have eclectic motivations to travel and take a gap year. A major reason may be social and institutional contexts, with education, peer and parents, employment, information accessibility and economic resources also influencing young travellers. Other motivations may include the desire to explore global cultures, cultivate new experiences and skills, contribute to society, and fulfill religious ideas, and the simple wish to take some time off (Jones 2004).

The TPB acted as a framework in exploring the influence that popular culture celebrity 'Bear' Grylls and his TV show *Man vs. Wild* had on the alternative tourism engagements and the beliefs, attitudes and behavioural intentions of the Gen-Y gapper participants. This model relied on the notion that all behaviour is rational whilst dismissing impulsive and creative action (Ham 2002). The TPB explains three factors that are essential to predicting behavioural intention (Ajzen 1985, 1991). The three factors include the individual's attitude towards the behaviour, the subjective norm and the perceived behavioural control. These factors determine behavioural intention, which generally predicts actual behaviours (Ham 2002). There are, however, a number of factors that disrupt this process known as external or intervening factors. These can include time, personality, resources or demographics.

The TPB operates under the following assumptions: beliefs give rise to attitudes that are consistent with these beliefs, attitudes give rise to intended behaviour that are consistent with these attitudes, and that behavioural intentions give rise to behaviours that are consistent with these intentions (Ham 2002). By utilising the TPB, this research initially investigated the research participants' beliefs, values and attitudes towards embracing specific popular culture forms. This included that of 'Bear' Grylls and his former TV show *Man vs. Wild*. How the respondents evaluated their connection with popular culture celebrities and how others might have perceived this relationship was considered. Finally, the perceived difficulty or ease that behavioural responses are performed with, as based on the individual's control beliefs, was explored. This approach recognised whether the participants were motivated to engage in some form of alternative tourism or nature driven experience because they associated with or consumed this form of popular culture.

Methodology

The research on which this paper is based aimed to highlight some areas where popular culture and alternative tourism can be valued as constructive factors influencing a Gen-Y group. Research associated with the social sciences will inevitably deal with people and their social behaviours. Given that this is a new area of research, this research design has taken an exploratory approach (Veal 2006). Five semi-structured in-depth interviews in this inductive and qualitative study were used to capture the respondents' meanings, definitions and descriptions of events relative to their own beliefs, values, motivations and behaviours (Minichiello et al. 1995). The participants were members of Gen-Y (born between 1980 and 1994) and had to have previously undertaken some form of alternative tourism. The respondents were required to know of popular culture celebrity 'Bear' Grylls and to have watched episodes from his TV show *Man vs. Wild*. This was particularly relevant when exploring how and why the respondents attached meaning to and organised themselves around popular culture and travel. It was also effective in identifying the influence and outcome of popular culture consumption on the beliefs, attitudes and behavioural intentions of the participants in accordance with the TPB (Ajzen 1985, 1991; Ham 2002).

The population of this study initially included anyone that could be classified as being part of Gen-Y. That is, subjects being born between 1980 and 1994 (Anderson 2009; McCrindle 2009). Purposive sampling organised the five respondents. It involved the deliberate selection of an informant due to the qualities that the participant possessed (Tongco 2007). The participants were sourced from the first authors' personal contacts.

All five participants of the study were male. This was largely due to the criteria required for the participants, in particular a knowledge of 'Bear' Grylls and his TV show *Man vs. Wild*. Respondents ranged in age from 20 to 26, with a mean of 23 years and were interviewed in Sydney in 2013.

In terms of content analysis and data collection, a three-step cyclical process took place. Using qualitative content analysis, these steps included:

- Manual theme and sub-theme codes matched to the literature and research objectives.
- Quotes and important examples to account for specific participant experiences identified.
- A continual process of comparison between the data and literature sources.

The interview transcripts were all read word-by-word to highlight any key words, phrases or emergent themes which were then coded. Codes included social norms, popular culture and everyday life, character traits of celebrities, 'Bear' Grylls and TV show *Man vs. Wild*, desire to do something, reflections from travel experiences, influence on beliefs, attitudes and behaviours.

Findings and discussion

From the five semi-structured interviews, a number of core themes emerged. They were applied to the TPB and the research objectives.

This study sought to understand the influence that popular culture, specifically the celebrity phenomenon, and alternative tourism engagements have on Gen-Y gappers. Popular culture consumption and alternative tourism engagements were highly dynamic fields and their association with the Gen-Y participants evoked sophisticated and nuanced results. The findings indicated that there was a degree of influence created by the celebrity 'Bear' Grylls and his TV show *Man vs. Wild* on many of the participants' motivations for travel or at least a nature-driven experience. However, the TPB showed this to be a limited relationship. The results established that the multifaceted nature of popular culture consumption and travel engagements required a more flexible model to explore its dynamics.

Section 1

Findings applied to the TPB.

Theme	Description of theme	Link to TPB
Popular culture shapes social and individual beliefs and attitudes	Popular culture influences the respondents' beliefs and attitudes on a social and personal level.	Beliefs give rise to attitudes that are consistent with these beliefs.
Subjective norms	The influence of 'others' – this includes peers, social norms, societal expectations and normative beliefs.	How do the respondents react to other groups and to what others may think?
Behavioural control	The way in which respondents perceive their abilities, skills and knowledge propels them towards a certain activity.	The perceived difficulty or ease with which individuals perform a behaviour or do something.
Behavioural intention	The person shows an intention to be proactive and/or engage in something.	This intention results from their beliefs, attitudes, subjective norms and behavioural controls.

In Theme 1, popular culture was acknowledged to be the norm that influences social and cultural trends. It was also viewed as a way to either fit in or avoid particular groups. The results found that social and individual factors influenced the participants' beliefs and attitudes towards consuming popular culture content. These social and individual variables acted as points of reference for the respondents to reflect upon themselves, others and social norms in society. One participant stated that:

> the influence of popular culture reflects the way I see human nature and a basic belief that I take as a given. (John)

Shane, Henry and Aaron believe that members of Gen-Y do not talk enough about the positive narratives associated with certain celebrities. Alternatively, John believed that a greater emphasis should be placed on the good deeds of the everyday person and not just on the actions of a specific celebrity. One participant mentioned that:

> Some people identify and concentrate on external and superficial features and forget to appreciate and embrace what is on the inside. (Aaron)

The respondents' beliefs and attitudes were shaped by individual factors. The endorsement of celebrities and popular culture in general created personalised connections. John acknowledged that:

> Stephen Fry and I happen to have the same liberal beliefs, which is probably one reason why I feel he would be a good role-model. His activism and willingness to admit when he made mistakes can inspire ... and it's always nice to feel less alone in the world. (John)

Theme 2, the subjective norm, considered how individuals perceive others viewing them. The results varied according to each respondent. Moreover, the medium of popular culture also altered the subjective norm for each participant. On the one hand, the respondents indicated that popular culture celebrities provide a point of discussion amongst their social groups. However, for some, celebrity endorsement is not just a social activity but also a personal one. Aaron maintained that:

> It does not matter to me what my peers think as to the celebrities I support. Everyone is entitled to their own beliefs. (Aaron)

Henry believes that popular culture reflects social norms. As he adopts the dress sense of famous celebrities in order to stand out more, he admitted to being influenced by trends. Shane believes that popular culture acts as a socialisation agent. He mentioned that:

> in some instances it does matter to me what my peers think about the celebrities I support ... but generally the people you get along with have similar tastes and interests. (Shane)

In terms of the Theme 3, celebrities, such as 'Bear' Grylls, strengthened some of the respondents' beliefs, abilities and knowledge when they were viewed as role models. Under this view, confidence levels were heightened and many of the participants boasted of a newly developed belief in themselves. Some participants noted that these role models influenced their view of the world and external issues outside of themselves. Henry noted the following:

> I have been inspired to hunt more (growing up in Norway), mainly through the influence of celebrities 'Bear' Grylls and Kristoffer Clausen. Bear Grylls constantly challenges himself which is a quality I admire. He inspires me the most through his documentary on the French Army Legion where he shows the existence of mind over body. I have also been in situations in the middle of the forest in Norway and had no idea of where I was and or where to go and I was able to get myself out of that situation. (Henry)

For Shane, John, Henry, Aaron and Sam, an important aspect to their elevated confidence and outlook was their previous travel experiences. Interestingly, for some participants, the combination of travel and the influence of vicarious role models strengthened their beliefs, knowledge and motivations. For example:

> Bear Grylls really highlights my love of the wilderness and remote environments. Through self-reflection and personal growth, while on the hikes, you become a better person and try your best to influence other people positively. (Shane)

In Theme 4, although not comprehensive, the findings still indicated that collective and individual beliefs and attitudes towards popular culture content may be key factors in shaping behavioural intentions. Media, in different forms, played an important role in delivering content and information to the participants. As opposed to traditional tourism promotional approaches, a number of studies have shown that films and television shows that do not directly concentrate on tourism promotion are more likely to generate interest in travel to a destination (Iwashita 2008). In reference to 'Bear' Grylls and his TV show *Man vs. Wild*, most of the respondents wanted to travel to remote places and experience different cultures. One participant stated that:

My personal experiences along with 'Bear' Grylls and his show have inspired me to participate in harder hikes, emulate some of the challenges he faces and put myself more out of my comfort zone. (John)

This section implicated the use of the TPB model. Due to its linear nature, this model suggested that the progression of popular culture, in the form of celebrity 'Bear' Grylls and his TV show *Man vs. Wild*, influenced the beliefs and attitudes of the participants. In turn, this model implied that popular culture motivated or affected the decisions of the respondents towards a nature based alternative travel experience. However, the connection between popular culture and alternative travel behaviours was not entirely supported by the interviews. This was because the TPB is only a model of process and the results from the interviews extended beyond its rigid framework. The model operates under the assumption that people are logical beings and that they take a systematic approach to process information. This would mean that their actions are always consistent with their beliefs (Fishbein and Manfrendo 1992; Ham and Weiler 2002). This model relies on the notion that all behaviour is rational, dismissing spontaneity and irrational actions (Ham 2002). Instead, a more comprehensive understanding of consumer culture is required. A 'macro perspective', as mentioned by McDonald and Wearing (2013), should be adopted as it acknowledges the diversity of popular culture within the context of consumer culture.

Section 2

This section explains findings that are relevant to the study's three research objectives.

Objective 1: To identify how popular culture celebrities influence the lives of Gen-Y gappers with the example of 'Bear' Grylls and his TV show *Man vs. Wild*.

Findings applied to Objective 1.

Theme	Description/sub-themes
Social and cultural influences	Popular culture provided: • Reinforcement and legitimisation of social and cultural norms • Social comfort and sense of belonging through shared meaning • Consuming the idea of connection
Identity and self-expression	Popular culture offered: • Personality reflections • Representations of the individual • Circumstances that shape perceptions (positive and negative) that reinforce identity
Self-enhancement	Popular culture provided: • Inspiration and motivation • Confidence in decision making • Opportunities to build and reinforce knowledge
Creative culture and multi-faceted experiences	Popular culture as a source for: • Knowledge • New experiences and opportunities • Entertainment • Adventure

Theme 1: social and cultural influences

The consumption of popular culture facilitated the creation of social connections (Cowen 2008; Dunlap and Johnson 2013). Commonly, popular culture was seen as a way to identify with or against social norms and provide stimuli for social conversations. Another socio-cultural factor that was recurrent was the belief that popular culture can help shape collective perceptions. Shane considered popular culture to be:

> Things that come and go with time, but for a moment in history people feel the need to conform to the populous to remain 'current'. (Shane)

For some of the participants, popular culture provided social comfort by creating a sense of connection and belonging to their peers. Participants' felt as though they shared a common interest or field of knowledge with their associated social groups. In fact, one participant mentioned the following:

> Popular culture can help one feel a sense of belonging to a specific social group. (Aaron)

Theme 2: identity and self-expression

Popular culture allowed identity conceptions to be formulated (Kellner 1991; Morton 2002; Noble, Haytko, and Phillips 2009). The content and brands associated with celebrities were noted as important factors in shaping the respondents perceptions of them. For a number of participants, having similar perceived values and beliefs with a celebrity or personality provided an additional reason to look at them for inspiration and motivation. John, in particular, claimed that:

> I have always maintained that I find individual acts more inspiring and motivating than a celebrity's beliefs or motto's. However I do recognise that 'Bear' Grylls is an important figure in many people's lives. I find his TV show *Man vs. Wild* to be both informative and entertaining which helps add to my existing interest for outdoor adventure, unique landscapes and challenging activities.

On the other hand, three participants clearly acknowledged how popular culture and celebrities also have a negative influence on society. These negative impacts were seen as prevalent and as manifesting in contemporary society. Shane supports this by stating that:

> How much is Gen-Y actually engaged in world politics … they say Gen-Y is more in-tune with world issues … and yet in contrast they obsess with trivial celebrities whose contribution to the world is battering their eyelashes. (Shane)

Theme 3: self-enhancement

The respondents noted that certain celebrities, such as 'Bear' Grylls, when viewed as role models, can stimulate self-enhancement. This was often due to the fact that some of the participants perceived similar values, beliefs and interests in the celebrity or vicarious role model. John claimed that:

> Bear strikes me as a calm and collected individual who is confident in his own abilities. His attitude to experiencing life, nature, and challenging yourself mentally and physically are inspirational attributes.

Theme 4: provides creative culture, entertainment and multi-faceted experiences

The participants engaged with and consumed popular culture as it provided pleasure and excitement whilst keeping them abreast of information and knowledge (Mankekar 2001; McCrindle 2009). Popular culture provided the majority of the participants with creative opportunities for culture and knowledge growth. It also offered entertainment and allowed for engagements with a variety of experiences. The popular culture medium, such as celebrities, TV shows, books and radio programs, provided these subjects with modes of escapism, novelty, information, comedy, ideas and/or the ability to connect with others.

In shaping personal and collective identities, popular culture helped a number of the participants make sense of the world and their interaction with others (Cowen 2008; Mankekar 2001). Popular culture enabled the respondents to define and realise their needs and articulate social differences with other individuals and groups in society (Mankekar 2001). According to Gamson (2001), many texts assume that the celebrity phenomenon is unquestionably superficial and unauthentic. Contrary to this preconception, this study has shown that celebrities, as vicarious role models, can act as socialisation agents and shape people's self-identity, aspirations and decision-making processes (Bush, Martin, and Bush 2004; Dix, Phau, and Pougnet 2010; Lockwood and Kunda 1997; Shuart 2007; Clark, Martin, and Bush 2001; Gavish, Shoham, and Ruvio 2010; Martin and Bush 2000). Krieken (2012) points out that the existing research regarding the notion of 'celebrity culture' rarely expands beyond the scope of media and cultural studies. The term 'celebrity society' in and of itself pays more attention to the social structuring of the celebrity phenomenon. This is because this term relates more inclusively to the way in which the celebrity is assigned, distributed, organised and responded to as a form of institutionalised social life.

Objective 2: To recognise the value and outcomes of alternative tourism engagements amongst the Gen-Y gappers.

Findings applied to Objective 2.

Theme	Description/sub-themes
Meaningful experiences	• Build identity and self-discovery • Self-efficiency (overcoming moments of hardship) • Develop interests, ambitions and values • Personal growth
Heightened awareness and discovery	• Global awareness and broadening of the mind • Discover cross cultural experiences • Reflections on the self, others and the world around them
Multi-faceted experiences	• Fosters respect for culture, nature, communities and adventure • Aesthetics • Escapism from urban settings • Excitement, fun and relaxation • Rich social interactions

Theme 1: meaningful experiences

Shane, John, Henry, Aaron and Sam all noted that their alternative travel experiences helped build their identity whilst also allowing for self-discovery. The respondents mentioned that they learnt most about themselves when they were forced to be self-reliant in the face of hardships during difficult hikes. One participant mentioned that:

> Going walkabout is an extremely self-reflecting activity ... the sense of individualism is awe inspiring. Introspection endows many positive outlooks for the future, in terms of your goals and aspirations in life. Having such a personal adventure makes you a better person ... you come home refreshed and with more knowledge then you left off. (Shane)

Having gone through physical and emotional trials, participants were able to reflect in hindsight about their experiences and accomplishments. This process of self-analysis enabled most of the respondents to develop, re-evaluate or even clarify their own interests, life ambitions and values.

Theme 2: heightened awareness and discovery

For the participants that backpacked around the world or hiked through wilderness areas, elements of opportunism, discovery, self-learning, personal growth and the recognition of other cultures were noted. All of the participants noted an increased level of global awareness. New found respect for the natural environment was joined by a consciousness and a heightened receptivity to other cultures. Henry established that:

> I have often found that people who have travelled are a more respectful to others. (Henry)

> It was an experience in a remote part of Romania last year where I referred to Bear Grylls for motivation. Whilst hiking I had reached a block in my path ... where an avalanche had destroyed the hiking track down this very steep stretch on a mountain. A moment of panic had beseeched me as I had to descend a 5-meter cliff with my backpack to the snow line. At that moment I thought about 'Bear' Grylls and how he always had faith in his skills to get himself out of hard situations. I knew I had the rock climbing skills to do it, and with that faith in myself I got down to the snow line and slowly made my way across to the other side of the avalanche chute. (Shane)

> From my hiking and hunting experiences I often drawn upon individualism and self-reliance ... I have been alone in the Norwegian mountains and forests and knew that I must take care of myself ... no one can help me even in rough situations and interactions with dangerous animals. (Henry)

Theme 3: multi-faceted experiences

All of the participants indicated that their travel expeditions provided them with a range of experiences. They most commonly commented on the perceived authenticity of their travel experiences and destinations. Many also referred to the sharing of stories with their friends, meeting down to earth people, relaxation and the excitement of their travels. As an outcome of their alternative tourism adventures, most of the participants cited their respect for global culture and nature. Aesthetics were key factors in the development of an appreciation for nature and the wilderness. In part, this is because the natural environment allowed for an escape from the perceived oppressive nature of urban settings. Shane and Henry recognised that:

> You can see real culture, real nature and get real excitement by going to remote isolated communities and environments. (Shane)

> I have so much more respect for nature and knowing how quickly things can change in the wilderness ... I recommend hiking to anyone as it provides many exciting moments. (Henry)

In experiencing remote natural environments first hand, away from urban settings, participants perceived themselves as having interacted with culture at an authentic level. In fact, the majority of the participants noted that alternative travel provided them with a different set of values and benefits over mainstream travel. For many of the participants, their engagements with alternative travel were acts of resistance against mass tourism and its associated conformities. This form of deviance can provide a sense of freedom from the constraints of authoritative figures and social norms (Wearing, McDonald, and Wearing 2013). Alternative travel consumption was valued as a more personalised, authentic and altruistic experience (Lyons and Wearing 2011; Wearing 2001). As deemed by the participants, travel is an important medium by which to gain wider experiences, discover self-identity and develop interests, ambitions, values and strengths (Lyons et al. 2012).

Objective 3: To identify how alternative travel experiences might influence future consumption motivations.

Findings applied to Objective 3.

Theme	Description/sub-themes
Opportunity for reflection	Alternative travel experiences provided: • Clarity, in terms of a clearer understanding of their relationship with and opinions regarding the consumption of popular culture • Reinforced and/or changed outlooks on popular culture and the celebrity phenomenon
Desire for future travel	Alternative travel experiences provided: • A source for personal development, exploration and excitement

Consumption, a mode of self-expression, is prevalent in everyday life (Campbell 2005). According to a postmodernist perspective, by consuming the values and messages associated with a celebrity's lifestyle, people are in fact consuming cultural symbols (Ritzer 2007). 'Bear' Grylls and his brand act as cultural symbols. According to the participants, these symbols represented adventure, challenges, survival, learning, outdoors, confidence, ambition and inspiration. The growth in the worldwide provisions of cultural content (Wearing, McDonald, and Wearing 2013) has helped facilitate a global consumption of his brand (Bear Grylls Ventures 2013; Grylls 2011). Nevertheless, the interviews have shown that there is more to this notion of valuing consumption for the sake of consuming (Ritzer 2007).

Theme 1: opportunity for reflection

Alternative tourism provided the participants with more opportunities to reflect on their own relationship with popular culture. Alternative tourism generated introspective moments for participants, with all subjects claiming that they were able to better evaluate society's affiliation with the celebrity phenomenon relative to their own beliefs. In this sense, alternative travel experiences provided these subjects with clarity. One participant stated that:

> It makes you realise how materialistic society can be. I have begun to buy less junk and started eating healthier foods, as a result of having travelled to developing countries such as Nepal and Tibet. (Aaron)

Alternative tourism engagements allowed all of the participants to either reinforce or change their personal views concerning the consumer society. In particular, hiking in the wilderness, hunting and backpacking around the world were instances that allowed for optimal self-reflection. Sam claimed that:

> In this era, we are highly dependent on gadgets. Hiking in the wilderness gives you a chance to experience purity in life. (Sam)

Respondents were asked to identify whether they believed that others in their generation held mistaken views regarding the celebrity society. In fact, all of the respondents believed that a broader view on how celebrity society influences people's lives must be adopted. John maintained that greater consideration should be placed on some of the lesser known figures in contemporary society as well as the good deeds of regular people. Celebrity society was seen as having both a surface value as well as a deeper meaning. Shane reflected upon this in the following:

> People need to realise that in many instances being a celebrity is a business. My generation is very quick to jump on the bandwagon without reflecting on why they follow this person or why they watch this show. Little to no time is spent on thinking how these people have an influence on them … especially in a positive way. (Shane)

Popular culture should be seen as vehicles for symbolic messages to the consumer and as a space in which creative cultural experiences can be augmented (Throsby 2008). Also, it should take into account the symbolic meanings attached to products and services, whereby the consumer specifically intends on using them in shaping an identity or lifestyle (Featherstone 1991).

Theme 2: desire for future travel

A number of the participants attributed their desire for further travel to their previous travel experiences. This was because travel was seen as being an extremely valuable source for personal development, exploration and excitement. Forms of alternative tourism, such as hiking in the wilderness or engaging with international cultures, were viewed by the participants as providing the greatest opportunity for clarity and as a means to achieve added perspective. Two participants stated the following:

> Travel changed my perceptions in life and now I am even keener to travel all around the world, help people and live a life that I desire. (Sam)

> I do wish to travel again someday as it is a very valuable learning experience and I feel because of it I am a different person. (John)

Conclusion

This study aimed to identify the influence that popular culture celebrities and alternative travel engagements have on Gen-Y gappers. The TPB was used as a model to identify whether the celebrity and role model 'Bear' Grylls and his TV show *Man vs. Wild* had an influence on the alternative tourism engagements and the beliefs, attitude and behavioural intentions of the research participants.

Findings indicated that identity construction was not based on a homogenous conception of popular culture. Rather, a diverse range of associations and participations with popular culture contributed towards the development of identity and the appreciation of dynamic socio-cultural relationships. This included modes of escapism, novelty, information, ideas and social connectivity. Celebrity approval influenced the self-identity and self-enhancement of the participants. This was discerned when celebrities were viewed as role models or when providing some form of motivation or inspiration (Bauman 2005; Bush, Martin, and Bush 2004; Krieken 2012; Shuart 2007). When evaluating the content and brand image of a celebrity and when choosing a role model to endorse, substance and authenticity were of primary importance. This was realised with the example of 'Bear' Grylls and his TV show *Man vs. Wild*. The participants of the study saw him as a positive role model that had impacted them in one way or another. He or his brand influenced them in terms of their self-assurance, self-discovery and their travel intentions.

The travellers experience has become increasingly unique, in the sense that travel has become more tailored for the individual traveller's needs (Sharpley and Stone 2012). By symbolically constructing meaning for the individual, travel critically goes beyond mere functionality (Østergaard and Jantzen 2000 cited in Smed 2012). Consuming new experiences through tourism related activities can be seen as a means of identity construction (Smed 2012). Having engaged in alternative tourism, such as hiking or trekking in the wilderness, the participants developed a greater respect and understanding of nature, social relations, cultures and communities. This in turn contributed to their sense of self. The aesthetics of the natural environment and escapism from urban settings facilitated these reflections and self-analyses (McDonald, Wearing, and Ponting 2009). In this form, the participants appreciated their alternative travel experiences for their true value and quality. This included opportunities for personal growth and increased global awareness.

Gen-Y represents a large segment in today's consumer population (Morton 2002; Noble, Haytko, and Phillips 2009). Their capacity for consumption holds significant implications for economic activity in the decades to come (Engebretson 2004). However, in today's highly concentrated market, marketers and advertisers acknowledge that new products directed towards this highly fragmented youth market requires additional targeted components (Dias 2003; Morton 2002). It necessitates some form of differentiation that resonates with Gen-Y and its subgroups. This is particularly true as the youth market assumes a large degree of control over the design, trends and nature of products and services produced nowadays (Campbell 2005; Morton 2002). As such, commodities have become a mechanism for marketers to adopt a wide range of cultural associations and illusions to appeal to their targeted groups (Featherstone 2007).

As a critical consumer group, Gen-Y claims to prefer brands with a core identity and with central values (Morton 2002). Driven by the consumer culture, consumption can provide people with a sense of identification and social connectivity (Cowen 2008). As an integral component to social life in modern western society, consumption has become a means to communicate self-identity (McDonald and Wearing 2013). In order to uphold popularity and maintain audience accessibility, many businesses, advertisers and marketers have realised the need for increased sophistication regarding the detailed dissemination of symbolic goods (Featherstone 2007). This enlarges our understanding of the complexities commonly associated with this generation, their consumption motivations and their decision-making processes (Noble, Haytko, and Phillips 2009).

Further research is required to attain a greater understanding of the diversity within this generation. Existing research on Gen-Y tends to be too general and needs to expand to accommodate the differences that exist amongst the individuals and the subgroups that make up this generation (Noble, Haytko, and Phillips 2009). Future research would benefit from including a larger sample size and a broader range of subjects from Gen-Y. However, as this was an exploratory study, quality and depth of information was prioritised with five participants. Nevertheless, a larger participant base would have allowed this research to make more generalisations representative of the population sample. The integration of female subjects would also have benefited this study. However, the focus on 'Bear' Grylls and his TV show *Man vs. Wild* largely contributed to a male-oriented participant group.

Rather than viewing popular culture and consumerism as a radicalised form of narcissism, it is important to analyse its form and content, image and narrative, all of which endorse the possibility of multiple connotations (Kellner 1991). Indeed, as reflected in the findings, popular culture consumption had both logical features and components that seemed to extend beyond the realm of the liner TPB. This is because the participants had more flexibility and creativity in their consumption motivations and behavioural intentions. This highlights the need to understand the consumption of popular culture from a broader and more inclusive perspective. This was seen in the participants' responses. They reflected on the motivating influence of the celebrity 'Bear' Grylls and his TV show *Man vs. Wild* on their individual identities, their developing self-awareness, their outlooks and their travel motivations. McDonald and Wearing point out that 'conducting an enquiry through the prism of consumer culture expands social psychological theories of self-identity because it not only describes the contemporary societal conditions in which it is formed, but it also provides insights into its origins' (2013, 122).

The notion of consumption has become a banal but, nevertheless, ubiquitous aspect of everyday life (McDonald and Wearing 2013). Despite its omniscience, according to Campbell (2005), the consumer's overall connection to consumer culture should not be seen as an entirely rational relationship. This paper suggests that a more comprehensive understanding of celebrity society and consumer culture is required. There is a tendency to disregard celebrity society and its social, cultural, political and economic role in society. Similarly, alternative tourism should also be valued as an activity that provides its participants with meaning and purpose. Tourism, in its many forms, is not immune from the consumer culture and the neoliberal agenda (Lyons et al. 2012; Munt 1994; Pretes 1995; Sharpley 2008). As the research findings have shown, specific forms of travel experiences that provide physical, emotional or intellectual benefits, such as hiking in the wilderness, may offer a heightened sense of satisfaction. As a consequence of their travel engagement, participants were able to better understand themselves, their consumption motivations and the world around them. Interacting with popular culture and engaging in any form of travel has become an inherent part of contemporary life. Consumption has become a way to communicate self-identity and discover as well as express a diverse set of social relationships.

References

Ajzen, I. 1985. "From Intentions to Actions: A Theory of Planned Behavior." In *Action Control: From Cognition to Behavior*, edited by J. Kuhl and J. Beckmann, 11–39. Berlin: Springer-Verlag.

Ajzen, I. 1991. "The Theory of Planned Behavior." *Organizational Behavior and Human Decision Processes* 50 (2): 179–211. doi:10.1016/0749-5978(91)90020-T.

Anderson, M. 2009. "Generation Change: Gen X, Gen Y and Baby Boomers – Hype or Risk?" *Change Drivers*. Accessed January 26, 2012. http://www.changedrivers.com.au/Articles/generational-change.htm.

Baudrillard, J. [1970] 1998. *The Consumer Society: Myths & Structures*. Thousand Oaks, CA: Sage.

Bauman, Z. 2005. *Liquid Life*. Cambridge: Polity Press.

Bear Grylls Ventures. 2013. "About." Bear Grylls Ventures (BGV). Accessed January 12. http://www.beargrylls.com/.

Beeton, S. 2005. *Film-induced Tourism*. Clevedon: Channel View.

Beeton, S. 2006. "Understanding Film-induced Tourism." *Tourism Analysis* 11 (3): 181–188. doi:10.3727/108354206778689808.

Benson, A. 2005. "Research Tourism: Professional Travel for Useful Discoveries." In *Niche Tourism: Contemporary Issues, Trends and Cases,* edited by M. Novelli, 133–142. Oxford: Elsevier Butterworth-Heinemann.

Bolan, P., S. Boy, and J. Bell. 2012. "We've Seen It in the Movies, Let's See If It's True: Motivation, Authenticity and Displacement in the Film-induced Tourism Experience." In *Contemporary Tourist Experience: Concepts and Consequences*, edited by R. Sharpley and P. R. Stone, 219–234. London: Routledge.

Boorstin, D. 1962. *The Image: A Guide to Pseudo-events in America*, New York: Atheneum.

Brown, L. 2009. "The Transformative Power of the International Sojourn: An Ethnographic Study of the International Student Experience." *Annals of Tourism Research* 36 (3): 502–521. doi: doi:10.1016/j.annals.2009.03.002.

Bull, G., A. Thompson, M. Searson, J. Garofalo, J. Park, C. Young, and J. Lee. 2008. "Connecting Informal and Formal Learning: Experiences in the Age of Participatory Media." *Contemporary Issues in Technology and Teacher Education* 8 (2): 100–107.

Bush, A. J., C. A. Martin, and V. D. Bush. 2004. "Sport Celebrity Influence on the Behavioral Intentions of Generation Y." *Journal of Advertising Research* 44 (1): 108–118. doi:10.1017/S0021849904040206.

Campbell, C. 2005. "The Craft Consumer: Culture, Craft and Consumption in a Postmodern Society." *Journal of Consumer Culture* 5 (1): 23–42. doi:10.1177/1469540505049843.

Celebrity Society. 2012. "Radio Program." *ABC Radio National*, September 5.

Christofi, V., and C. L. Thompson. 2007. "You Cannot Go Home Again: A Phenomenological Investigation of Returning to the Sojourn Country after Studying Abroad." *Journal of Counseling & Development* 85 (1): 53–63. doi:10.1002/j.1556-6678.2007.tb00444.x.

Clark, P. W., C. A. Martin, and A. J. Bush. 2001. "The Effect of Role Model Influence on Adolescents: Materialism and Marketplace Knowledge." *Journal of Marketing Theory and Practice* 9 (4): 27–36.

Cowen, T. 2008. "Why Everything Has Changed: The Recent Revolution in Cultural Economics." *Journal of Cultural Economics* 32 (4): 261–273. doi:10.1007/s10824-008-9074-y.

Cushner, K., and A. Karim. 2004. "Study Abroad at the University Level." In *Handbook of Intercultural Training*, edited by D. Landis, M. Bennett, and J. Bennett, 289–308. 3rd ed. Thousand Oaks, CA: Sage.

Dearden, P., and S. Harron. 1992. "Tourism and the Hill Tribes of Thailand." In *Special Interest Tourism*, edited by B. Weiler and C. M. Hall, 95–104. London: Belhaven Press.

Dias, L. P. 2003. "Generational Buying Motivations for Fashion." *Journal of Fashion Marketing and Management* 7 (1): 78–86. doi:10.1108/13612020310464386.

Discovery Channel. 2013. *Man vs. Wild*. Accessed May 12. http://dsc.discovery.com/tv/man-vs-wild/.

Discovery Channel Australia. 2013. *Man vs. Wild*. Accessed May 12. http://www.discoverychannel.com.au/shows/manvs.wild.

Dix, S., I. Phau, and S. Pougnet. 2010. "Bend It Like Beckham: The Influence of Sports Celebrities on Young Adult Consumers." *Young Consumers: Insight and Ideas for Responsible Marketers* 11 (1): 36–46.

Dunlap, R., and C. W. Johnson. 2013. "Consuming Contradiction: Media, Masculinity and (Hetero) Sexual Identity." *Leisure/Noir* 37 (1): 69–84. doi:10.1080/14927713.2013.783728.

Eadington, W. R., and V. L. Smith. 1994. "Introduction: The Emergence of Alternative Forms of Tourism." In *Tourism Alternatives: Potentials and Problems in the Development of Tourism*, edited by V. L. Smith and W. R. Eadington, 1–12. Sussex: John Wiley & Sons.

Elsrud, T. 1998. "Time Creation in Travelling: The Taking and Making of Time among Women Backpackers." *Time & Society* 7 (2–3): 309–334. doi:10.1177/0961463X98007002008.

Engebretson, J. 2004. "Odd Gen Out." *American Demographics* 26 (4): 11–12.

Escalera, K. W. 2012. "Generation Y: Luxury's Most Buoyant Market." *Luxury Society*. Accessed July 16, 2013. http://luxurysociety.com/articles/2012/05/generation-yluxurys-most-buoyant-market.

Featherstone, M. 1991. *Consumer Culture and Postmodernism*. London: Sage.

Featherstone, M. 2001. "Consumer Culture." In *International Encyclopedia of the Social & Behavioral Sciences*, edited by N. J. Smelser and P. B. Baltes, 2662–2669. Amsterdam: Elsevier.

Featherstone, M. 2007. *Consumer Culture and Postmodernism*. Los Angeles, CA: Sage.

Fishbein, M., and M. J. Manfredo. 1992. "A Theory of Behavior Change." In *Influencing Human Behavior*, edited by M. J. Manfredo, 29–50. Champaign, IL: Sagamore.

Frost, W. 2009. "From Backlot to Runaway Production: Exploring Location and Authenticity in Film-induced Tourism." *Tourism Review International* 13 (2): 85–92. doi:10.3727/154427209789604570.

Gamson, J. 2001. "The Assembly Line of Greatness: Celebrity in Twentieth-century America." In *Popular Culture: Production and Consumption*, edited by C. L. Harrignton and D. D. Bielby, 259–282. Malden, MA: Blackwell.

Gavish, Y., A. Shoham, and A. Ruvio. 2010. "A Qualitative Study of Mother-adolescent Daughter-vicarious Role Model Consumption Interactions." *Journal of Consumer Marketing* 27 (1): 43–56. doi:10.1108/07363761011012949.

Grylls, B. 2011. *Mud, Sweat and Tears*. London: Transworld.

Ham, S. 2002. "Putting Communication Theory Into Practice: Influencing Visitor Behaviour Through Interpretation." In *Report on Queensland Parks and Wildlife Service Persuasive Communication Workshop*, edited by P. Harmon-Price, 35–44. Brisbane: Queensland Parks and Wildlife Service.

Ham, S. H., and B. Weiler. 2002. "Interpretation as the Centrepiece of Sustainable Wildlife Tourism." In *Sustainable Tourism: A Global Perspective*, edited by R. Harris, T. Griffin, and P. Williams, 35–44. Oxford: Butterworth-Heinemann.

Harrington, C. L., and D. D. Bielby, eds. 2001. *Popular Culture: Production and Consumption*. Malden, MA: Blackwell.

Higgins-Desbiolles, F. 2008. "Justice Tourism and Alternative Globalisation." *Journal of Sustainable Tourism* 16 (3): 345–364. doi:10.1080/09669580802154132.

Hirschorn, S., and K. Hefferon. 2013. "Leaving It All Behind to Travel: Venturing Uncertainty as a Means to Personal Growth and Authenticity." *Journal of Humanistic Psychology* 53 (3): 283–306. doi:10.1177/0022167813483007.

Howe, N., and W. Strauss. 2000. *Millennials Rising: The Next Great Generation*. New York: Vintage Books.

Hudson, S., and J. B. Ritchie. 2006. "Film Tourism and Destination Marketing: The Case of Captain Corelli's Mandolin." *Journal of Vacation Marketing* 12 (3): 256–268. doi:10.1177/1356766706064619.

Hudson, S., Y. Wang, and S. M. Gil. 2011. "The Influence of a Film on Destination Image and the Desire to Travel: A Cross-cultural Comparison." *International Journal of Tourism Research* 13 (2): 177–190.

IMDb (International Movie Data Base). 2013. "Man vs. Wild." *IMDb.* Accessed September 13. http://www.imdb.com/title/tt0883772/?ref_=ttep_ep_tt.

Iwashita, C. 2008. "Roles of Films and Television Dramas in International Tourism: The Case of Japanese Tourists to the UK." *Journal of Travel & Tourism Marketing* 24 (2–3): 139–151. doi:10.1080/10548400802092635.

Johnson, C. W., L. Richmond, and B. D. Kivel. 2008. "' What a Man Ought to Be, He Is Far From': Collective Meanings of Masculinity and Race in Media." *Leisure/Loisir* 32 (2): 303–330. doi:10.1080/14927713.2008.9651412.

Jones, A. 2004. *Review of Gap Year Provision.* London: Department for Education and Skills.

Jones, A. M. 2005. "Assessing International Youth Service Programmes in Two Low Income Countries." *Voluntary Action: The Journal of the Institute for Volunteering Research* 7 (2): 87–100.

Kacen, J. J., and J. A. Lee. 2002. "The Influence of Culture on Consumer Impulsive Buying Behaviour." *Journal of Consumer Psychology* 12 (2): 163–176. doi:10.1207/S15327663JCP120 2_08.

Kellner, D. 1991. "Popular Culture and the Construction of Postmodern Identities." In *Modernity and Identity,* edited by S. Lash and J. Friedman, 141–177. Oxford: Blackwell.

Kerwin, A. M. 2012. "Millennials with Money? Find Out Where They Live and How They Spend." *Advertising Age.* Accessed July 16, 2013. http://adage.com/article/news/affluent-millennials-live-spend/238679/.

Kim, H., and S. L. Richardson. 2003. "Motion Pictures Impacts on Destination Images." *Annals of Tourism Research* 30 (1): 216–237. doi:10.1016/S0160-7383(02)00062-2.

Kivel, B. D., and C. W. Johnson. 2009. "Consuming Media, Making Men: Using Collective Memory Work to Understand Leisure and the Construction of Masculinity." *Journal of Leisure Research* 41 (1): 109–133.

Krieken, R. V. 2012. *Celebrity Society.* London: Routledge.

Lanfant, M. F., and N. H. H. Graburn. 1992. "International Tourism Reconsidered: The Principle of the Alternative." In *Tourism Alternatives: Potentials and Problems in the Development of Tourism,* edited by V. L. Smith and W. R. Eadington, 88–112. Sussex: John Wiley & Sons.

Lim, L. L. K., M. W. Chou, and T. C. Melewar. 2008. "Do You Know Y? Mobile Internet and the Thumb Generation." *International Journal of Technology Marketing* 3 (2): 137–152. doi:10.1504/IJTMKT.2008.018861.

Lipsitz, G. 2001. *Time Passages: Collective Memory and American Popular Culture.* Minneapolis: University of Minnesota Press.

Lockwood, P., and Z. Kunda. 1997. "Superstars and Me: Predicting the Impact of Role Models on the Self." *Journal of Personality and Social Psychology* 73 (1): 91–103. doi:10.1037/0022-3514.73.1.91.

Lundberg, C., and M. Lexhagen. 2012. "Bitten by the Twilights Saga: From Pop Culture Consumer to Pop Culture Tourist." In *Contemporary Tourist Experience: Concepts and Consequences,* edited by R. Sharpley and P. R. Stone, 147–164. London: Routledge.

Lury, C. 1996. *Consumer Culture.* Oxford: Blackwell.

Lury, C. 2011. *Consumer Culture.* 2nd ed. New Brunswick, NJ: Rutgers University Press.

Lyons, K., J. Hanley, S. Wearing, and J. Neil. 2012. "Gap Year Volunteer Tourism: Myths of Global Citizenship?" *Annals of Tourism Research* 39 (1): 361–378. doi:10.1016/j.annals.2011.04.016.

Lyons, K. D., and S. Wearing. 2008. "Volunteer Tourism as Alternative Tourism: Journeys beyond Otherness." In *Journeys of Discovery in Volunteer Tourism: International Case Study Perspectives,* edited by K. D. Lyons and S. Wearing, 3–11. Wallingford: CABI.

Lyons, K., and S. L. Wearing. 2011. "Gap Year Travel Alternatives: Gen-Y, Volunteer Tourism and Global Citizenship." In *Tourism and Demography,* edited by K. A. Smith, I. Yeoman, C. Hsu, and S. Watson, 101–116. London: Goodfellow.

Maddux, W. W., and A. D. Galinsky. 2009. "Cultural Borders and Mental Barriers: The Relationship between Living Abroad and Creativity." *Journal of Personality and Social Psychology* 96 (5): 1047–1061. doi:10.1037/a0014861.

Mankekar, P. 2001. "Popular Culture." In *International Encyclopedia of the Social and Behavioural Sciences*, edited by N. J. Smelser and P. B. Baltes, 11733–11737. Stanford, CA: Elsevier.

Martin, A. J. 2010. "Should Students Have a Gap Year? Motivation and Performance Factors Relevant to Time Out after Completing School." *Journal of Educational Psychology* 102 (3): 561–576. doi:10.1037/a0019321.

Martin, C. A., and A. J. Bush. 2000. "Do Role Models Influence Teenagers Purchase Intentions and Behaviors?" *Journal of Consumer Marketing* 17 (5): 441–453. doi:10.1108/07363760010341081.

McCrindle, M. 2002. *Understanding Generation Y.* North Parramatta, NSW: The Australian Leadership Foundation. Accessed March 4, 2013. http://www.learningtolearn.sa.edu.au/Colleagues/files/links/UnderstandingGenY.pdf.

McCrindle, M. 2009. *The ABC of XYZ – Understanding the Global Generations.* Sydney: University of New South Wales Press.

McDonald, M., and S. Wearing. 2013. *Social Psychology and Theories of Consumer Culture.* Sussex: Routledge.

McDonald, M. G., S. Wearing, and J. Ponting. 2009. "The Nature of Peak Experience in Wilderness." *The Humanistic Psychologist* 37 (4): 370–385. doi:10.1080/08873260701828912.

McRobbie, A. 1994. *Postmodernism and Popular Culture.* London: Routledge.

Mieczkowski, Z. 1995. *Environmental Issues of Tourism and Recreation.* Lanham: University Press of America.

Millington, K. 2005. "Gap Year Travel – International." *Travel & Tourism Analyst* 12:1–50.

Minichiello, S., R. Aroni, E. Timewell, and L. Alexander. 1995. *In-depth Interviewing.* 2nd ed. Longman: Frenchs Forest.

Montuori, A., and U. Fahim. 2004. "Cross-cultural Encounter as an Opportunity for Personal Growth." *Journal of Humanistic Psychology* 44 (2): 243–265. doi:10.1177/0022167804263414.

Morton, L. P. 2002. "Targeting Generation Y." *Public Relations Quarterly* 47 (2): 46–48.

Mowforth, M., and I. Munt. 2003. *Tourism and Sustainability: Development and New Tourism in the Third World.* New York: Routledge.

Müller, D. K. 2006. "Unplanned Development of Literary Tourism in Two Municipalities in Rural Sweden." *Scandinavian Journal of Hospitality and Tourism* 6 (3): 214–228. doi:10.1080/15022250600667433.

Munt, I. 1994. "The 'Other' Postmodern Tourism: Culture, Travel and the New Middle Classes." *Theory, Culture and Society* 11 (3): 101–123. doi:10.1177/026327694011003005.

Noble, S. M., D. L. Haytko, and J. Phillips. 2009. "What Drives College-age Generation Y Consumers?" *Journal of Business Research* 62 (6): 617–628. doi:10.1016/j.jbusres.2008.01.020.

Novelli, M., ed. 2005. *Niche Tourism: Contemporary Issues, Trends and Cases.* Oxford: Butterworth Heinemann.

Nusair, K., A. Bilgihan, F. Okumus, and C. Cobanoglu. 2013. "Generation Y Travellers Commitment to Online Social Network Websites." *Tourism Management* 35: 13–22. doi:10.1016/j.tourman.2012.05.005.

Patterson, B. 2007. "A-Z of Generation Y." *Herald Sun.* Accessed July 8, 2013. http://www.heraldsun.com.au/news/sunday-heraldsun/a-z-of-generation-y/story-e6frf92f-1111113909372.

Pearce, D. 1994. "Alternative Tourism: Concepts, Classifications, and Questions." In *Tourism Alternatives: Potentials and Problems in the Development of Tourism*, edited by V. L. Smith and W. R. Eadington, 15–30. Sussex: John Wiley & Sons.

Pintrich, P. R. 2003. "Motivation and Classroom Learning." In *Handbook of Psychology: Educational Psychology*, W. M. Reynolds and G. E. Miller, 103–122. Hoboken, NJ: Wiley.

Prensky, M. 2001. "Digital Natives, Digital Immigrants." *On the Horizon* 9 (5). Accessed February 17, 2014. http://www.nnstoy.org/download/technology/Digital%20Natives%20-%20Digital%20Immigrants.pdf. doi:10.1108/10748120110424816.

Pretes, M. 1995. "Postmodern Tourism: The Santa Claus Industry." *Annals of Tourism Research* 22 (1): 1–15. doi:10.1016/0160-7383(94)00026-O.

Richards, G., and J. Wilson. 2004. "The International Student Travel Market: Travelstyle, Motivations, and Activities." *Tourism Review International* 8 (2): 57–67. doi:10.3727/1544272042782183.

Richards, G., and J. Wilson. 2005. "Youth Tourism: Finally Coming of Age?" In *Niche Tourism: Contemporary Issues, Trends and Cases*, edited by M. Novelli, 39–46. Oxford: Routledge.

Ritzer, G. 2007. *The Globalization of Nothing*. 2nd ed. Thousand Oaks, CA: Pine Forge Press.

Sellnow, D. D. 2010. *The Rhetorical Power of Popular Culture: Considering Mediated Texts*. Thousand Oaks, CA: Sage.

Sharpley, R. 2008. *Tourism, Tourists and Society*. 4th ed. Huntington: ELM.

Sharpley, R., and P. R. Stone, eds. 2012. *Contemporary Tourist Experience: Concepts and Consequences*. London: Routledge.

Shearer, E. 2002. "Generation Ignored: Medill's Washington Program Learned That the Media Can Reach Young Readers, If Only They'd Try." *American Journalism Review* 24 (3): 7.

Shuart, J. 2007. "Heroes in Sport: Assessing Celebrity Endorser Effectiveness." *International Journal of Sports Marketing & Sponsorship* 8 (2): 126–140.

Simpson, K. 2005. "Dropping Out or Signing Up? The Professionalisation of Youth Travel." In *Working the Spaces of Neoliberalism: Activism, Professionalisation and Incorporation*, edited by N. Laurie and L. Bondi, 447–469. Malden, MA: Blackwell.

Smed, K. M. 2012. "Identity in Tourist Motivation and the Dynamics of Meaning." In *Contemporary Tourist Experience: Concepts and Consequences*, edited by R. Sharpley and P. R. Stone, 130–146. London: Routledge.

Stebbins, R. A. 2009. *Leisure and Consumption: Common Ground/Separate Worlds*. Hampshire: Palgrave Macmillan.

Swanson, M. A. 1992. "Ecotourism: Embracing the New Environmental Paradigm." Paper presented at the International Union for Conservation of Nature and Natural Resources (IUCN) IVth World Congress on National Parks and Protected Areas, Caracas, Venezuela, February 10–21.

Swarbrooke, J., and S. Horner. 2007. *Consumer Behaviour in Tourism*. 2nd ed. Oxford: Butterworth-Heinemann.

Throsby, D. 2008. "The Concentric Circles Model of the Cultural Industries." *Cultural Trends* 17 (3): 147–164. doi:10.1080/09548960802361951.

Tongco, M. D. C. 2007. "Purposive Sampling as a Tool for Informant Selection." *Ethnobotany Research & Applications* 5: 147–158.

Veal, A. J. 2006. *Research Methods for Leisure and Tourism: A Practical Guide*. 3rd ed. Essex: Pearson Education.

Wattchow, B., and M. Brown. 2011. *A Pedagogy of Place: Outdoor Education for a Changing World*. Victoria: Monash University.

Wearing, S. 2001. *Volunteer Tourism: Experiences That Make a Difference*. Wallingford: CABI.

Wearing, S. L., M. McDonald, and M. Wearing. 2013. "Consumer Culture, the Mobilisation of the Narcissistic Self, and Adolescent Deviant Leisure." *Leisure Studies* 32 (4): 367–381.

Wearing, S., and J. Neil. 2009. *Ecotourism: Impacts, Potentials, and Possibilities*. 2nd ed. Oxford: Butterworth-Heinemann.

Wearing, S. L., and J. Ponting. 2009. "Breaking Down the System: How Volunteer Tourism Contributes to New Ways of Viewing Commodified Tourism." In *The Sage Handbook of Tourism Studies*, edited by T. Jamal and M. Robinson, 254–268. London: Sage.

Weaver, D. B., and L. J. Lawton. 2007. "Twenty Years On: The State of Contemporary Ecotourism Research." *Tourism Management* 28 (5): 1168–1179. doi:10.1016/j.tourman.2007.03.004.

Wheeller, B. 1993. "Sustaining the Ego." *Journal of Sustainable Tourism* 1 (2): 121–129. doi:10.1080/09669589309450710.

Williamson, A. 2008. "Gen-Y." *Teacher: The National Education Magazine*, ACER, May, 60–61.

Wolburg, J. M., and J. Pokrywczynski. 2001. "A Psychographic Analysis of Generation Y College Students." *Journal of Advertising Research* 41 (5): 33–50.

World Tourism Organisation (WTO). 2008. *Youth Travel Matters – Understanding the Global Phenomenon of Youth Travel*. Madrid: UNWTO. Accessed June 10, 2013. http://www.siimt.com/work/sites/siimt/resources/LocalContent/1172/6/YouthTravel_protec.pdf.

Index

For Product Safety Concerns and Information please contact our EU
representative GPSR@taylorandfrancis.com Taylor & Francis Verlag GmbH,
Kaufingerstraße 24, 80331 München, Germany

Batch number: 08153807

Printed by Printforce, the Netherlands